Elite • 163

Special Operations Forces in Afghanistan

Leigh Neville • Illustrated by Ramiro Bujeiro

Consultant editor Martin Windrow

First published in Great Britain in 2008 by Osprey Publishing,
Midland House, West Way, Botley, Oxford OX2 0PH, UK
443 Park Avenue South, New York, NY 10016, USA

A CIP catalog record for this book is available from the British Library

ISBN: 978 1 84603 310 0

Edited by Martin Windrow
Page layout by: Ken Vail Graphic Design, Cambridge, UK
Index by Glyn Sutcliffe
Typeset in Helvetica Neue and ITC New Baskerville
Originated by PPS Grasmere, Leeds, UK
Printed in China through World Print Ltd.

08 09 10 11 12   10 9 8 7 6 5 4 3 2 1

FOR A CATALOG OF ALL BOOKS PUBLISHED BY OSPREY MILITARY AND
AVIATION PLEASE CONTACT:

NORTH AMERICA
Osprey Direct, c/o Random House Distribution Center, 400 Hahn Road,
Westminster, MD 21157
E-mail: info@ospreydirect.com

ALL OTHER REGIONS
Osprey Direct UK, P.O. Box 140 Wellingborough, Northants, NN8 2FA, UK
E-mail: info@ospreydirect.co.uk

Osprey Publishing is supporting the Woodland Trust, the UK's leading
woodland conservation charity, by funding the dedication of trees.

www.ospreypublishing.com

Dedication

This work is dedicated to my late grandfather, WO2 Edward
A. Farrelly, who lit the fire; and to the men and women who
have served, and continue to serve, in both Operation
'Enduring Freedom' and the International Security
Assistance Force – guys, this one's for you.

Author's note

Some locations mentioned in this text have deliberately
been kept vague, as have some specific operational details
which may impact on Coalition tactics, techniques and
procedures. Some unit names, locations and roles have
also been omitted or altered for reasons of operational
security.

Acknowledgments

Many of the contributors to this work cannot be named
as they continue to work in the special operations or
intelligence fields; so, to 'JZW', 'A', 'Dax', 'J', 'HD', 'ISD',
'Jim' and the other 'anonymous by necessity' folks who
assisted me – thank you so much. I would also like to thank
Mathew R, Keith W, Paul B, Rolf H and Kathy and Eddie S
for their continued support.

Artist's note

Readers may care to note that the original paintings from
which the colour plates in this book were prepared are
available for private sale. All reproduction copyright
whatsoever is retained by the Publishers. All inquiries
should be addressed to:
Ramiro Bujeiro, CC 28, 1602 Florida, Argentina

The Publishers regret that they can enter into no
correspondence upon this matter.

AMF Militia locally recruited by Coalition forces
ANA Afghan National Army
CAG Combat Applications Group (1st SF Operational
Detachment – Delta, US Army)
CENTCOM US military command responsible for Middle East
& Central Asia
CJC-MOTF Coalition Joint Civil-Military Operations Task Force
CJSOTF Combined Joint Special Operations Task Force
CJTF-M Combined Joint Task Force – Mountain
COS *Commandement des Opérations Spéciales* (coordinating
entity for all French military SOF, similar to USSOCOM &
British SF Directorate)
CTC Counter Terrorist Center (of US Central Intelligence Agency)
DA direct action (combat missions, as opposed to intelligence-
gathering)
DEVGRU US Naval Special Warfare Development Group
ISAF International Security Assistance Force (NATO)
JIATF-CT Joint Interagency Task Force - Counterterrorism
JSOC Joint Special Operations Command (US)
HALO High Altitude Low Opening (parachute jump)
HVT High Value Targets (enemy leadership)
ODA, ODB, ODC Operational Detachments Alpha, Bravo,
Charlie (US Army Special Forces)

OEF Operation 'Enduring Freedom' (umbrella codename for
US/Coalition forces in Afghanistan, distinct from ISAF)
'OGA' 'Other Government Agency' (US military slang for CIA)
OP observation post
SAD Special Activities Division (of US CIA)
SAM Surface-to-air missile
SAS Special Air Service (British)
SASR Special Air Service Regiment (Australian)
SEAL Sea, Air, Land (US Navy SOF units)
SF Special Forces (US Army)
SFSG Special Forces Support Group (British airborne force
providing back-up for SF operations, e.g. security cordons
and QRF)
SMU Special Mission Unit
SOAR Special Operations Aviation Regiment (US Army)
SOF special operations forces (generic term)
SOPs Standard operating procedures
SOTG Special Operations Task Group (Australian)
SR surveillance & reconnaissance
SSE sensitive site exploitation
UKSF United Kingdom Special Forces (British)
USSOCOM United States Special Operations Command (joint
services coordinating entity for all military SOF)

SPECIAL OPERATIONS FORCES IN AFGHANISTAN

INTRODUCTION

An 'operator' from a US Army Special Forces Operational Detachment Alpha (ODA) poses for a pre-mission photo. Over civilian clothing he wears the SPEAR RBA (Special Operations Forces Equipment Advanced Requirements, Ranger Body Armor) plate-carrier with woodland-pattern cover; this is compatible with the MOLLE load-bearing pouch equipment. The weapon is a Mk 11 Mod 0 semi-automatic 7.62mm sniper rifle – basically an enhanced-accuracy 7.62mm version of the venerable M16. Readers should note that in all non-publicly released images throughout this book, all faces and identifying characteristics of special operators have been digitally obscured, for reasons of personal security. (Courtesy 'JZW')

'One of my first and lasting memories was my trip from Kandahar airfield into the city for the first time. We were in the Toyota trucks, rolling 'hard' because they had been getting hit a lot. That meant we had an extra AMF in the back and we went windows-down with muzzles out. I was a bit nervous, and didn't want to make any mistakes in front of the Team guys.

'The grizzled SF veteran who had been briefing me on their team's SOPs wasn't making me any calmer ... I remember as we were leaving the base he turned back to me and said "There's one more requirement if you're gonna ride in our truck ... you gotta like Creedence"; then he put in a cassette of CCR's greatest hits. The nervousness melted right away, and I was calm and tapping my foot as I cruised into Kandahar for the first time to the sound of classic rock. I'll never forget it. That was Afghanistan.' *US Army special operator, Afghanistan*

Afghanistan is a land that has rarely known peace. The 19th century saw bloody defeats inflicted on the British and their Indian Army in both the First (1838–42) and Second (1878–80) Anglo-Afghan Wars. During and since the 1979–89 occupation by Soviet forces in an attempt to shore up a communist regime, Afghanistan has been fought over by rival governments, factions, tribes and warlords. In fact, these particular episodes of widely reported turmoil have differed only in degree, and not in nature, from the pattern of life that that region has known over many centuries: warfare in Afghanistan is essentially based on ethnic or communal rivalries rather than modern ideological quarrels.

The defining moment in the country's modern history, which sowed the seeds for all later events, was the Soviet invasion in 1979.[1] Installing a puppet government under Babrak Karmal in the capital, Kabul, the Soviets boasted that they would eliminate the anti-communist *mujahideen* (fighters) in a few short months. But those local fighters would receive massive covert support from the West, and active reinforcement by Islamic volunteers from many countries. Ten years later the Soviets withdrew, after suffering anything from 35,000 to 50,000 troop deaths and up to three times that number of other casualties. The experience thoroughly demoralized the Soviet Army for a decade thereafter, and released many thousands of physically and psychologically crippled veterans into a society that itself proved to be on the verge of political collapse.

[1] See Men-at-Arms 178, *Russia's War in Afghanistan*

The 'Afghan Arabs' and the Taliban

During the 1980s the loosely aligned Afghan mujahideen groups were reinforced by the so-called 'Afghan Arabs', an eventual 30,000 volunteers from across the Islamic world, fuelled by the Koranic imperative to *jihad*. Amongst these was a man whose name would rise to notorious prominence in later years – Usama bin Laden. The wealthy Saudi son of a construction magnate, bin Laden developed an Islamic charity to support the Afghan Arabs. This organization, centred on a guesthouse for foreign fighters over the Pakistani border in Peshawar, became known as *al Qaeda* or 'the Base'. Blooded in the Soviet-Afghan War, many of these volunteers went on to fight in other conflicts involving Islamic peoples, from Kashmir and Chechnya to Kosovo.[2]

In the vacuum left by the departing Soviets, the mujahideen factions fought against the ailing central government before its inevitable collapse in 1992. Hope for a new central government was short-lived, as the seven major mujahideen factions descended into a bitter civil war for control of the country. These struggles naturally extended southwards over the political border into and beyond the so-called Tribal Territories along Pakistan's north-west frontier; vast numbers of Afghans had fled across the borders during the Soviet occupation, and the notional powers of the Pakistani government over the Tribal Territories were exercised only covertly.

The Taliban

The Taliban arose in 1994 from a small group of Pashtun religious students *(talibs)* in southern Afghanistan. Under the leadership of the one-eyed cleric Mullah Muhammad Omar the Taliban became a popular movement, railing against the brutal excesses of the rival warlords and

---

[2] See Elite 146, *The Yugoslav War (2)*

the corruption spread by the ubiquitous opium trade. Their solution, however, was to bring the country under their own Dark-Age interpretation of *sharia* law; supported by Pakistani intelligence (the ISI), the Taliban movement grew quickly.

Bin Laden returned to Afghanistan in 1996 after being forced to leave his refuge in Sudan. He brought with him a cadre of al Qaeda fighters, and soon attracted many Afghan Arab veterans. As a gift to Mullah Omar, Bin Laden donated vehicles, built roads, and recruited the largest jihadist army of modern times – al Qaeda's Brigade 055 – which Bin Laden deployed against the *Shura Nazar* or Northern Alliance of anti-Taliban groups.

Everything changed on 11 September, 2001. Two days before the terrorist attacks which killed 2,973 people in New York, Virginia and Pennsylvania, Ahmad Shah Masoud, the leader of the Northern Alliance, was assassinated in his headquarters in the Panjshir Valley in a suicide bombing by two al Qaeda terrorists posing as journalists. Al Qaeda had eliminated the United States' closest ally in Afghanistan.

In the aftermath of '9/11' America received pledges of military support from many nations, from the United Kingdom, Australia, New Zealand and Canada to France. Indeed, on 12 September, for the first time in history, NATO invoked Article 5 of its founding charter providing for mutual protection of member states against attack; this paved the way for NATO participation, and the eventual deployment to Afghanistan of the International Security Assistance Force (ISAF).

'Jawbreaker'

The first US ground forces to set foot inside Afghanistan did so a scant 15 days after '9/11'. This small team, codenamed 'Jawbreaker,' inserted covertly from the former Soviet airbase of Karshi-Khandabad (K2) in Uzbekistan, where a formidable US presence was building, and landed in the Panjshir Valley in a Russian-built but CIA-operated Mi-17 helicopter in the pre-dawn darkness of September 26. These eight men were not members of any military unit, but of the Central Intelligence Agency's paramilitary Special Activities Division (SAD) and Counter Terrorist Center (CTC). To the men of the Special Forces, they would be known colloquially by the acronym OGA – 'Other Government Agency'.

Consisting of former special operators, communications and linguistics experts, the team brought with them satellite communications enabling their 'ground truth' intelligence reports to be available instantly to headquarters staff at CIA Langley and Central Command (CENTCOM), the military command responsible for Operation 'Enduring Freedom' (OEF) – the forthcoming US/Coalition operations in Afghanistan. Jawbreaker also carried 3 million dollars in US currency in non-sequential $100 bills, which would be used to shore up Northern Alliance support to OEF.

The Jawbreaker team facilitated the planned insertion of the first US Army Special Forces detachments with Northern Alliance commanders; assessed potential air targets for CENTCOM; provided an in-country combat search-and-rescue (CSAR) capability; and would provide bomb-damage assessments for the coming air campaign.

OPERATION 'ENDURING FREEDOM'

Operation 'Enduring Freedom' began officially on the evening of 6 October, 2001 with Operation 'Crescent Wind' – the Coalition air campaign targeting Taliban command-and-control and air defence facilities. Most of the Taliban's ageing SA-2 and SA-3 SAMs, along with their attendant radar and command units, were destroyed on the first night of operations, as were their small fleet of MiG-21 and SU-22 aircraft.

With the threat of high-altitude SAMs negated and total air dominance quickly established, aerial targeting soon focused on Taliban infrastructure, leadership and troop targets, as well as known al Qaeda facilities. These targets were struck by a range of USAF, USN and British RAF aircraft types, including the venerable B-52H and the B-1B long-range bombers along with the AC-130 Spectre, operating from bases at K2 and in Pakistan. The way was now clear for deployments on the ground. The structure of the special operations forces committed to OEF was basically as follows:

Under the overall leadership of Gen Tommy Franks, Coalition Forces Commander, CENTCOM, four major task forces were initially dedicated to OEF: the Combined Joint Special Operations Task Force (CJSOTF); Combined Joint Task Force-Mountain (CJTF-Mountain); the Joint Interagency Task Force-Counterterrorism (JIATF-CT); and the Coalition Joint Civil-Military Operations Task Force (CJCMOTF).

CJSOTF comprised three subordinate task forces: Joint Special Operations Task Force – North (JSOTF-North), known as Task Force Dagger; Joint Special Operations Task Force – South (JSOTF-South), aka Task Force K-Bar; and the secretive Task Force Sword (later Task Force 11).

ODA operators meet with Gen Tommy Franks in October 2001. Note the *pakol* hats, Mk 11 sniper rifle (left), and M4A1 carbine fitted with a sound suppressor and the ACOG 4x optical sight. (USSOCOM/DOD photo)

Initial SOF structure, Operation 'Enduring Freedom'

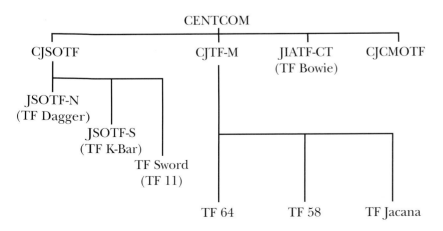

Task Force Dagger

JSOTF-North, led by Col John Mulholland, was formed around his 5th Special Forces Group, with integral air assets from the 160th Special Operations Aviation Regiment (SOAR). Dagger was assigned to the north of Afghanistan, and tasked with infiltrating Special Forces ODA (Operational Detachment Alpha) teams to advise and support the warlords of the Northern Alliance. These ODAs were generally composed of a Special Forces A Team supported by an Air Force Special Tactics team, and worked jointly with CIA assets already on the ground.

The Army Special Forces' motto *De Oppresso Liber* ('To Liberate the Oppressed') hints at one of the key skills of Army SF- Foreign Internal Defense (FID): infiltrating foreign countries and raising, training and advising indigenous guerrilla forces. Within the 13-man ODA teams each SF operator has a different primary specialty, from demolitions to communications to engineering, but is cross-trained in others. Several ODAs are supported by an ODB (Operational Detachment Bravo), which provides intelligence product, medical and logistical support to the ODAs. Both the ODB and the ODAs are led by an ODC (Operational Detachment Charlie), generally an SF battalion command element. The ODAs are also supported by integrally attached USAF Special Tactics operators – usually Combat Controllers (CCTs) trained to guide close air support. Some ODAs, particularly if tasked with direct action (DA) missions, may also be supported by USAF Pararescue Jumpers, who are specialist combat medics.

Task Force K-Bar

JSOTF-South, TF K-Bar, was led by Navy SEAL Capt Robert Harward, and formed around a core of Navy SEAL Teams 2, 3 & 8 and the Army's 1st Bn/3d SF Group. The SEALs are structured in 16-man platoons, six of which comprise a SEAL Team. Platoons in OEF were most often deployed in sensitive site exploitation (SSE) or DA missions, while four-man sub-elements were assigned to surveillance and reconnaissance (SR) operations. The SEALs are generally considered to be more focused on direct action when compared with the unconventional warfare and FID focus of Army SF. K-Bar nevertheless concentrated on SSE and SR taskings, although some 3d SF Group ODAs were deployed in the FID role alongside 5th SF Group. K-Bar was additionally the home for several SOF units from other Coalition nations, including the German *Kommando Spezialkräfte* (KSK), Canada's Joint Task Force 2 (JTF-2), and New Zealand's 1st Special Air Service Group (NZSAS).

Task Force Sword

TF Sword/ TF 11 was the JSOC's so-called 'hunter-killer' force, with the mission of capturing or killing senior leadership or 'high-value targets' (HVTs) in both al Qaeda and Taliban. Sword was structured around a two-squadron component of Special Mission Unit (SMU) operators from the Combat Applications Group (CAG) and the Naval Special Warfare Development Group (DEVGRU), supported by Ranger security teams, and the intelligence specialists of Grey Fox, NSA and the CIA.

CAG – 1st SF Operational Detachment-Delta – are modelled on the British 22nd Special Air Service Regt (22SAS), and are the US Army's primary direct action, hostage rescue and special reconnaissance unit.

The three Squadrons (A, B and C) are each divided into three Troops – two dedicated to DA and one Recce Troop. In OEF they were often known obliquely as 'Task Force Green'; the Rangers who worked in support of Sword were TF Red, DEVGRU were termed TF Blue, Grey Fox TF Orange, and the 160th SOAR were TF Brown.

DEVGRU are the former SEAL Team 6, which grew from a maritime counterterrorist unit into a sort of naval equivalent of CAG. They are structured in a similar manner to the Army unit, with specialist DA and recce elements, and the two units are considered somewhat interchangeable by JSOC.

Grey Fox are the most secretive of the JSOC units; they are trained and equipped to gather actionable intelligence for the SMUs through electronic (ELINT) and signals (SIGINT) methods, along with the more traditional human intelligence (HUMINT). They were also experienced at 'man-hunting', having helped target and capture HVTs in the Balkans, Somalia and Colombia.

Coalition SOF were sometimes attached to Sword to support specific operations; UK Special Forces (UKSF), particularly the Special Boat Service (SBS), were generally integrated and attached for the longer term. One US special operations source explained to the author that in the early months only US and UK SF played any major roles in TF 11

In rugged mountain terrain, this MH-60K Pave Hawk from the 160th SOAR crash-landed in a stream bed. The helicopter was stripped of sensitive equipment, and later destroyed from the air. (Courtesy 'JZW')

operations; other Coalition troops were used predominantly in SR and some SSE missions. Another added: 'There was a lot of "hey, there's a war, and everyone wants to come" going on back then – only we were running the show, and needed to be the ones that nailed the big bad guys for the press.'

CJTF-Mountain

CJTF-M also initially comprised three subordinate commands: TF 64 – a special operations task force built around a squadron of the Australian Special Air Service Regt (SASR); the USMC TF 58, of the 15th Marine Expeditionary Unit (MEU) – which was replaced in January 2002 by TF Rakkasan (formed of components of the 101st Airborne and 10th Mountain divisions, along with 3rd Bn Princess Patricia's Canadian Light Infantry, and TF Jacana, a battle group of 1,700 British personnel built around 45 Commando, Royal Marines.

JIATF-CT

Also known as TF Bowie, the JIATF-CT was an integrated intelligence entity manned by personnel from all OEF participating units, both US and Coalition, and civilian agencies. Led by BrigGen Gary Harrell, one of the most experienced special operators in theater, TF Bowie established the Coalition's interrogation facility at Bagram air base and provided intelligence product to the CJSOTFs. At its largest, Bowie numbered 36 US military personnel, 57 from civilian agencies such as the FBI, NSA and CIA, and officers from Coalition SOF, including UKSF and SASR.

Embedded within Bowie, but reporting to TF Sword, was Advanced Force Operations (AFO), a 45-man contingent of CAG recce specialists augmented by SEALs from DEVGRU and supported by Grey Fox. AFO had the mandate of 'intelligence preparation of the battlefield'; they conducted covert SR operations for both Bowie and Sword, and would prove instrumental in Operation 'Anaconda' (see below).

Operators in a typical Afghan mountain village. The soldier wears SPEAR armor, and just visible on his left upper arm is a diamond-shaped infrared-reflective patch for nighttime 'identification-friend-or-foe'. (Courtesy 'JZW')

A mounted SF patrol halts to talk with locals. They are travelling in an up-armored HMMWV mounting a Mk 19 automatic grenade-launcher (AGL), and finished in field-expedient camouflage of closely applied small brown 'curls' on khaki. (Courtesy 'JZW')

CJCMOTF

CJCMOTF was eventually headquartered in Kabul but with two geographically divided subordinate commands: Civil-Military Operations Center North, and Civil-Military Operations Center South. They had responsibility for managing OEF civil support and humanitarian efforts, which evolved in 2002 into the Provincial Reconstruction Team (PRT) concept; some 34 teams are now operational.

OPERATIONS OCTOBER–DECEMBER 2001

Special Forces ODAs

As the aerial campaign continued, TF Dagger were planning to insert their first teams into Afghanistan from K2. Aviators from the 2d Bn of the 'Nightstalkers' – the Army's 160th SOAR – maintained their MH-47E Chinooks and MH-60Ls on 'strip alert', awaiting a break in the bad weather to allow the helicopters to negotiate safely the notorious Hindu Kush mountains.

After two weeks of preparatory aerial bombardment, the first two SF ODAs were infiltrated into Afghanistan in the evening and early hours of 19/20 October, 2001. The first team to touch down was the 12-man ODA 555, who linked up with Jawbreaker in the Panjshir Valley and were taken to a safe house to meet representatives of warlord Fahim Khan, the successor to Masoud as military commander of the Northern Alliance. They began operations alongside Khan's forces the very next day.

The weather that night had been dangerous enough to force the two MH-60L Direct Action Penetrators (DAPs) flying escort for the MH-47E carrying the second SF team, ODA 595, to turn back to K2. As well as a

The famous image of a USAF Combat Controller (CCT) attached to ODA 555 ('Triple Nickel') riding with Northern Alliance forces in October/November 2001. The local method of transport posed challenges for the American ODAs; few had extensive riding experience, and the traditional wooden Afghan saddles were far from comfortable. This led to one of the most unusual resupply requests to TF Dagger – for civilian-manufactured Cordura saddles, which were duly airdropped to their location. This photo appears to have been taken before their arrival. (DOD photo)

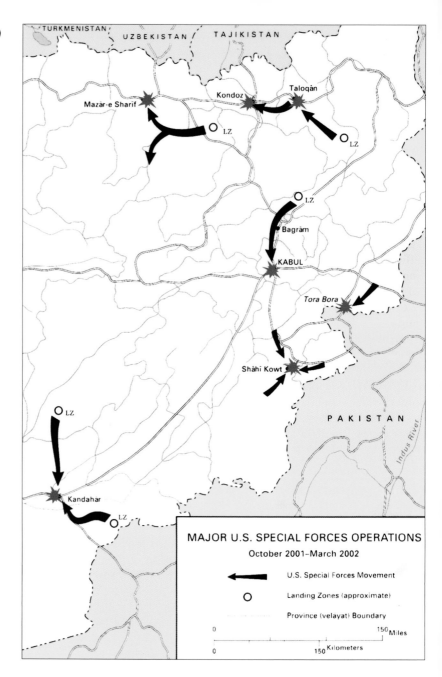

MAJOR U.S. SPECIAL FORCES OPERATIONS
October 2001–March 2002

→ U.S. Special Forces Movement

○ Landing Zones (approximate)

Province (velayat) Boundary

potentially deadly ice build-up on their rotors, and the treacherous 16,000-foot peaks, the aviators found they had to contend with a night-time sandstorm on the way into Afghanistan. But despite the appalling conditions, the Chinook crew managed to complete their mission, touching down at 2am local time in the Dari-a-Souf Valley just south of the regional capital of Mazar-e-Sharif. ODA 595 was met at the landing zone by the militia of ethnic Uzbek warlord Gen Abdur Rashid Dostum, commander of the largest Northern Alliance faction. Dostum held a strong powerbase around Mazar-e-Sharif and was an accomplished political intriguer: he had previously allied himself with, and later betrayed, the Soviets, their Kabul puppet government and the Taliban.

The Kandahar raids

Meanwhile, in southern Afghanistan, another special operation was under way. Some 200 Army Rangers from 3d Bn/75th Ranger Regt, with airmen from the 23d Special Tactics Sqn (STS), conducted a combat drop from MC-130P Combat Talons onto a remote airstrip southwest of the city of Kandahar.

Preceded by a small Army Pathfinder team, the Rangers met minimal Taliban resistance and the location, codenamed Objective 'Rhino', was quickly secured. The parachute drop and airstrip seizure were filmed, and later some grainy night-vision footage was televised by the Pentagon as proof that US forces could operate in any location within Afghanistan – a strong psychological message to the Taliban. The Ranger mission also paved the way for the later use of the airstrip as Forward Operating Base (FOB) Rhino by the Marines of 15th MEU. No casualties were suffered in the actual operation, but two Rangers assigned to the CSAR element supporting the mission died when their MH-60K crashed in Pakistan (the result of a 'brown out' rather than enemy action).

Concurrently, another much less publicized mission was being conducted outside Kandahar; this remains classified, but its aim was to capture or kill Taliban HVTs. It was launched from the USS *Kitty Hawk* (which was serving as a floating SOF base in the Indian Ocean). The ground elements were drawn from JSOC's Combat Applications Group and supported by teams from 23d STS. The Kandahar target was one of Taliban leader Mullah Omar's residences and, although Omar was

Members of an ODA moving on foot over the unforgiving terrain of the Afghan mountains. (Courtesy 'JZW')

Rangers of the 3/75th took part in the Kandahar raids of winter 2001/02. This soldier, part of a security cordon for an ODA patrol, wears the issue MICH helmet with night-vision goggle mount, desert BDUs, but woodland-pattern issue kneepads. His M4A1 is fitted with the M68 Aimpoint sight and AN/PEQ-2 IR illuminator. The light object on the front of his left shoulder is several chemical glow-sticks attached to the equipment straps of his SPEAR RBA. (Courtesy 'JZW')

absent, intelligence material was recovered. As the CAG team prepared to extract, Taliban forces approached the compound and engaged them with small arms and rocket-propelled grenades. The CAG operators returned fire, breaking contact under suppressive fire from an orbiting AC-130 gunship, and successfully exfiltrated on helicopters from the 160th SOAR.

Officially, casualties were described as 'light', but rumours point to multiple casualties amongst the operators. CAG had planned to insert a 'stay-behind' SR team in the area, but was frustrated by the Taliban response. A possible piece of evidence for the ferocity of the contact is that a wheel assembly from an MH-47E was torn off as it struck a compound wall during the extraction; the Taliban, unsurprisingly, used the wheel as a propaganda opportunity, claiming it as evidence of a shot-down US helicopter.

The Northern Alliance
While TF Sword carried out the Kandahar raids, ODA 595 was striking up a productive relationship with Gen Dostum in the north. The ODA had split into two elements, Alpha and Bravo; Alpha rode on horseback with Dostum to his headquarters, to plan the impending attack on Mazar-e-Sharif, while Bravo, tasked with clearing the Dari-a-Souf Valley, travelled into the Alma Tak mountains to begin preparations.

On 20 October the team guided in the first JDAM (Joint Direct Attack Munition) 'smart bomb' from an orbiting B-52H. Dostum was suitably impressed – 'You made an aircraft appear and drop bombs. General Dostum is very happy!' (Quoted in the ARSOF history, *Weapon of Choice*.) Dostum was soon taunting his Taliban opponents over their radio frequencies – a curious aspect of the war between the Taliban and the Northern Alliance, and a crude example of psychological warfare: 'This is General Dostum speaking. I am here, and I have brought the Americans with me!'

The US conducted their own Psyops, with EC-130E Commando Solo aircraft beaming radio transmissions in both Dari and Pashto dialects to the Afghan civilian population. Aircraft also dropped huge numbers of leaflets decrying the Taliban and al Qaeda as criminals, and promoting the $25 million reward placed on bin Laden's head.

The ODA 595 Bravo team were coordinating their own airstrikes in the Dari-a-Souf Valley, cutting off and destroying Taliban reinforcements and frustrating their attempts to relieve their embattled forces in the north. Cumulatively, the airstrikes showed increasing results as the Taliban began to withdraw towards Mazar-e-Sharif. Dostum's riders and the ODA 595 Alpha team followed, pausing only to direct further air support.

On the Shomali Plains, ODA 555 and an OGA team with Fahim Khan's forces began calling in air on entrenched Taliban positions at the southeastern end of Bagram air base. The Alpha team set up an observation post (OP) in an air traffic control tower, using it as a base for their AN/PEQ-1 SOFLAM (Special Operations Forces Laser Marker), and guiding in two 15,000lb BLU-82 Daisy Cutters which devastated the Taliban lines.

By 5 November the advance of Dostum and his horsemen was stalled at the Taliban-held village of Bai Beche in the strategically vital Dari-a-Souf Valley, where two Northern Alliance attacks had been driven back. While ODA 595 organized close air support, Dostum prepared his men to follow up the bombing with a cavalry charge; this was mistimed, and 250 Uzbek cavalry charged the Taliban lines exactly as the B-52 made its final approach to bomb them. An operator with ODA 595 is quoted in Max Boot's *War Made New:*

'Three or four bombs hit right in the middle of the enemy position. Almost immediately after the bombs exploded, the horses swept across the objective — the enemy was so shell-shocked. I could see the horses blasting out the other side. It was the finest sight I ever saw. The men were thrilled; they were so happy. It wasn't done perfectly, but it will never be forgotten'. The political fall-out from a serious 'friendly fire' tragedy might have severed Dostum's relationship with the Americans – a relationship that was the key to their goals in northern Aghanistan; thankfully, fate dealt a lucky hand and the cavalry charge succeeded, breaking the back of the defence (see Plate E).

Other ODAs were now inserting at regular intervals. On 23 October ODA 585 was infiltrated near Konduz to assist the warlord Burillah Khan. On 2 November the ten-man ODA 553 inserted into the Bamian Valley with Gen Kareem Kahlili's forces; and ODA 534 got into the Dari-a-Balkh Valley (after being delayed by poor flying conditions) to support Gen Mohammed Atta, a sometime associate of Gen Dostum and head of the Jaamat-e-Islami militia. An operator with ODA 534 recalled:

'The team was finally able to infil northern Afghanistan by Chinook on the night of November 2 after several days of bad weather. If the helo insertion failed, an airborne operation was scheduled for the following evening. In addition to the 12-man ODA and two Air Force CCTs, three Agency officers were attached. The Agency team consisted of a case

A Toyota Hilux pickup used by SOF, with an M240B light machine gun on a jury-rigged mount, and field-expedient wooden lockers added for ammo and other gear. (Courtesy "JZW")

officer/Dari linguist, a former SEAL officer, and a former SF [medical] officer. The team was met on the HLZ by Atta's forces and an Agency CTC officer [from Jawbreaker] who had infiltrated two weeks prior and had been working with Dostum. He now took command of the Agency team, while the rest of his group and another ODA [595] remained with Dostum and his men. The ODA team leader's Russian did come in handy once the RON site was reached and the team split, but the primary [interpreter] between the team and Atta and his men was the Agency case officer.'

ODAs 586 and 594 were brought into the country on 8 November in MH-47s, and picked up on the Afghan/Tajik border by CIA Mi-17s; 586 deployed into Konduz with the forces of Gen Daoud Khan, and 594 into the Panjshir to assist ODA 555.

Mazar-e-Sharif

ODA 534 moved through the Dari-a-Souf with Atta's militia, and linked up with Dostum and ODA 595 outside of Mazar-e-Sharif to develop a plan of attack against the Taliban-held city. At the critical Tangi Pass, the gateway from the Balkh Valley to Mazar-e-Sharif, Taliban forces were dug in to halt the Alliance's rapid advance. On 9 November ODAs 595 and 534 positioned themselves in mountainside hides and began calling in airstrikes against these entrenched defenders. The Taliban responded with indirect fires from BM-21 rockets; these were quickly silenced by the B-52H, and Northern Alliance forces – on foot, on horseback, in pickups and in captured BMP armored personnel carriers – raced toward the gates of the city. On 10 November Mazar-e-Sharif fell to the Alliance, providing the first hint that the war might not be the year-long affair predicted by the Pentagon. Civil Affairs Teams (CAT) from the 96th Civil Affairs Bn and Tactical Psyop Teams (TPT) from the 4th Psychological Operations Group, both assigned under TF Dagger, were immediately deployed into Mazar-e-Sharif to assist in winning the hearts and minds of the inhabitants.

In the central northern region, ODA 586 were advising Gen Daoud Khan outside of Taloqan, and coordinating Coalition airstrikes, when the general launched a surprise infantry assault. Before the first bomb could be dropped, Taloqan fell on 11 November.

The Rangers of 3/75 carried out their second combat drop in Afghanistan on the night of 13 November, when a platoon-sized element, accompanied by eight men from the 24th STS, dropped into a site southwest of Kandahar codenamed 'Bastogne', to secure a FARP (Forward Air Refuelling Point). MC-130s soon landed at the improvised strip and deposited four AH-6J Little Birds from the 160th, which launched an attack on targets around Kandahar. With their mission completed the Little Birds returned, reloaded onto MC-130s, and the combined team flew off into the night.

Kabul, Konduz and Kandahar

Three days after the fall of Mazar-e-Sharif, Kabul was captured by Gen Fahim Khan and the men of ODA 555; surviving Taliban and al Qaeda retreated toward Kandahar and Tora Bora. On 14 November, ODA 574 inserted into the southern village of Tarin Kowt in four MH-60Ks, bringing with them the future President of Afghanistan, the Pashtun leader Hamid Karzai.

As the cities fell in rapid succession, TF Dagger's attention became focused on the last northern Taliban stronghold – Konduz. Daoud Khan and ODA 586 used massive airstrikes to demoralize the Taliban defenders, and after 11 days of continual aerial bombardment Daoud took the traditional Afghan step of opening negotiations with his enemies, successfully securing the Taliban's surrender on 23 November.

On 25 November the establishment of FOB Rhino near Kandahar added further pressure on the beleaguered Taliban. A three-man SEAL team conducting a reconnaissance before the Marines landed were mistakenly engaged by orbiting AH-1W Cobras, but thankfully suffered no casualties. The 15th MEU landed a battalion-size force at Rhino, and was soon reinforced by the newly arrived Australian SASR squadron.

Hamid Karzai began moving on Kandahar with ODA 574, gathering fighters among local Pashtuns until his militia eventually numbered some 800. They fought for two days against Taliban dug into ridgelines overlooking the strategic Sayd-Aum-Kalay bridge, before seizing the bridgehead and opening the road to Kandahar. Tragedy struck on 5 December when a 2,000lb JDAM landed among this force, killing three members of the ODA and seriously

An SF soldier at Bagram air base; note civilian cap and clothing, SPEAR armor and load-bearing equipment in woodland-pattern camouflage. His M4A1 has the ACOG sight, and a Safariland pistol holster is worn on a drop strap and two thigh straps. (Courtesy 'JZW')

wounding five; more than 20 of Karzai's militiamen were killed and Karzai himself was slightly wounded in the blast. An ODA operator explained to the author that the accident occurred due to unfamiliarity with the PLGR, a precision lightweight GPS receiver widely used for navigation and targeting: 'When the PLGR batteries go dead and you put new ones in, it defaults to showing the GPS location of itself. The TACP with 574 wasn't trained for that; [he] put new batteries in, looked at the unit, and called the GPS location in to the bird; the bird asked for confirmation because the data had changed since last call, and 574 confirmed that it was correct – at which time they dropped the JDAM'. Along with a Marine casevac CH-53, ODB 570 and ODA 524 were deployed by helicopter to assist with evacuating the wounded and to replace the fallen operators of 574. The following day, Karzai successfully negotiated the surrender of both the remaining Taliban forces around Sayd-Aum-Kalay and of the entire city of Kandahar. ODA 524 and ODB 570 mounted up with Karzai's militia and began the final push.

Another SF team were also fighting their way towards Kandahar: ODA 583 had infiltrated into the Shin Narai Valley, southeast of the city, to support Gul Agha Sherzai, its former governor. By 24 November the ODA had established OPs which allowed them to call airstrikes on Taliban positions at Kandahar airport, weakening them every day. On 7 December, Sherzai's forces seized the airport and, informed of the surrender of the Taliban in Kandahar, entered the city, soon followed by Karzai.

The campaign had taken just under two months – 49 days – from the insertion of the first ODA teams to the fall of Kandahar. It was accomplished by several hundred SOF and perhaps 100 OGA, supported by their determined allies of the Northern Alliance and the awe-inspiring might of United States air power.

Tora Bora

After the fall of Kabul, al Qaeda elements – allegedly including bin Laden and other leadership figures – withdrew to the eastern city of Jalalabad, capital of Nangarhar province. Jalalabad was only a short distance from Tora Bora, the network of cave systems and defences developed by the mujahideen during their war against the Soviet occupiers. Tora Bora lies in the White Mountains, only just over 12 miles from the border, where a crossing point at Parachinar leads into Pakistan's Northwest Frontier province. The area was familiar to bin Laden; he had spent time there with the mujahideen in the 1980s, and knew that the mountain caverns would provide the perfect stronghold – one that the Soviets had never managed to conquer fully.

Coalition signals and human intelligence suggested that significant numbers of al Qaeda fighters and possible high-value targets were moving from Jalalabad to take refuge in Tora Bora. Due to resistance from the higher echelons of both the US government and military to committing conventional forces on the ground (in the misplaced fear of replicating the Soviet experience), a decision was made to attack Tora Bora using SOF supporting local militia. ODA 572 and a small group of SAD operators were deployed to advise Eastern Alliance forces under the control of two warlords – Hazrat Ali and Mohammed Zaman, who nursed a deep-seated mutual dislike. Eventually some 2,500 to 3,000 Afghan Militia Forces (AMF), paid for by the CIA, were recruited for the operation to isolate and destroy al Qaeda elements using Tora Bora as a sanctuary.

The leader of the CIA Jawbreaker team requested the 3/75th Rangers (who were at that time deployed to Pakistan in support of TF Sword) to act as stop groups along escape routes from Tora Bora, but the JSOC commander denied the request. The logistics, particularly in terms of helicopter lift capability, would have been difficult, although both the Jawbreaker leader and USMC Gen James Mattis believe that using Rangers to seal the trails might have succeeded. It must also be remembered, however, that up until Tora Bora the use of AMF militias supported by ODAs had been consistently successful.

At the onset of the attack ODA 572, with their attached CCT, called in precision airstrikes including by B-52Hs, while the Afghan militias attacked al Qaeda positions with varying degrees of enthusiasm. According to ODA members, the militias would gain ground initially, only to relinquish these gains later the same day. At one point ODA 572 was going to be extracted due to the militias' reluctance to press the attack.

With 5th SF Group and Jawbreaker stretched thin across the country, JSOC was tasked to assist, and on 10 December, 40 operators from B Sqn CAG arrived at Tora Bora. Small teams attached themselves to local commanders, and took over tactical command from the CIA. Advised by ODA, CAG and CIA operators, the militias eventually started to make some halting progress; but on 12 December, Mohammed Zaman (incredibly) opened negotiations with the al Qaeda forces in Tora Bora. Much to the frustration of the SOF, a truce was called until 8am the next morning 'to allow al Qaeda forces time to agree a surrender amongst themselves'.

This appears to have been a transparent ruse: several hundred al Qaeda members (some estimate up to 1,000), including men of Brigade 055, escaped during the night along the mountain paths towards

Pakistan. It has also been alleged, by both Afghan and US SOF sources, that members of the CIA-funded militias acted as guides for bin Laden's fighters; one rumour indicates a payment of US $6 million made to Hazrat Ali to shepherd the al Qaeda leadership to safety. Gary Berntsen, leader of the CIA team at Tora Bora, believes that two large al Qaeda groups escaped: one of 135-odd personnel headed east into Pakistan, while bin Laden, with 200 Saudi and Yemeni jihadists, took the snow-covered route through Parachinar.

Eventually, around 17 December, the battle drew to a close. Indications were that several hundred al Qaeda members had been killed and just under 60 captured at Tora Bora. Across the border, Pakistani Border Scouts, allegedly assisted by members of JSOC and the CIA, captured upward of another 300 foreign fighters. ODA 561 was brought in on 20 December to support 572 in conducting SSEs of the cave complexes, and to take DNA samples from the al Qaeda bodies.

Zhawar Kili

In January 2002 another series of caves used by al Qaeda were discovered in Zhawar Kili, just south of Tora Bora, and airstrikes were called in before ground elements were infiltrated. A SEAL platoon accompanied by a German KSK and a Norwegian SOF team spent nine days conducting an SSE, clearing the estimated 70 caves and 60 structures in the area and recovering a huge amount of intelligence materials and munitions.

OPERATION 'ANACONDA', 2002

Order of battle, Operation 'Anaconda', March 2002:

Task Force DAGGER
ODAs, 5th SF Group (Airborne)
Co B, 2d Bn/160th SOAR
Combat Tactical Air Controllers, AFSOC
Afghan Militia Forces (AMF)
Task Force HAMMER (Commander Zia)
Task Force ANVIL (Cdrs Kamil Khan & Zakim Khan)

Task Force RAKKASAN
3d Bde, 101st Abn Div (Air Assault)
1st & 2d Bns/187th Infantry
1st Bn/87th Inf, 10th Mountain Div

Task Force COMMANDO
2d Bde, 10th Mountain Div
4th Bn/31st Inf
3d Bn/ Princess Patricia's Canadian Light Inf

Task Force 64
1 Sqn, Australian SASR
Task Force K-BAR
ODAs, 3d SF Group (Abn)
Task Force BOWIE
Advanced Force Operations
Task Force SWORD/11
Mako 30, 31 & 21, Task Force Blue

In February 2002 an SF intelligence analyst working for TF Bowie identified patterns in intelligence product that led him to believe that surviving al Qaeda forces were massing in the Lower Shah-e-Khot Valley, 60 miles south of Gardez. The Lower Shah-e-Khot bordered the Pakistani Tribal Territories into which many al Qaeda fighters were believed to have escaped during the battle for Tora Bora. Other personnel within TF Dagger, the AFO and the OGA were making the same connections. The analysis by TF Bowie, supported by HUMINT from the OGA and SIGINT from NSA, indicated that perhaps 150 to 200 al Qaeda fighters were harboring in the valley, with the strong possibility of leadership targets also being present. An operation was soon in the planning, to be known as 'Anaconda'. Initially three AFO teams (two from CAG and one from a DEVGRU recce troop) were infiltrated into OPs around the valley to provide real-time 'eyes on' intelligence to the planners. The DEVGRU team (callsign Mako 31) discovered an al Qaeda position, complete with 12.7mm DShK heavy machine gun, nestled in the same location that they had selected for their OP; this was the first of several ominous signs.

The plan evolved around Task Force Hammer and TF Anvil, an *ad hoc* grouping of Afghan militia led by three ODAs (394, 372 & 594), and supported by a collection of AFO types and an Australian SASR patrol. Hammer would enter the Shah-e-Khot to flush out the al Qaeda believed to be hiding in

Local AMF riding in a white pickup – note the typical multicolored decorative touches across the top of the tailgate. They wear a mixture of American woodland BDUs and local copies of British DPM, and are armed with AKs and the ever-present RPG-7. The commitment of AMF groups against strong dug-in opposition around the Shah-e-Khot Valley for Operation 'Anaconda' proved to be premature. (Courtesy 'JZW')

the small villages dotted across the valley floor, while Anvil would act as a blocking force to seal off the escape routes. Several SASR teams from TF 64, along with other Coalition SOF, would also establish outer cordon covert OPs, to call in air on any retreating al Qaeda.

Into the Shah-e-Khot

Conventional forces – the 'Rakkasans', of 3d Bde, 101st Abn Div and 1st/87th Inf of 10th Mtn Div – would be committed in their first major operation, air-assaulting into the valley from Chinooks supported by six AH-64 Apaches. The infantry were to take up blocking positions inside the valley to cut off escape from the villages. Late-breaking CIA HUMINT alleging that the al Qaeda forces were living on the peaks surrounding the valley rather than down in the villages was apparently overlooked by the planners.

The operation was launched on 2 March 2002, and immediately ran into problems: TF Hammer had difficulty driving their trucks under blackout conditions over the muddy tracks into the Shah-e-Khot. Hammer halted to await the planned preparatory aerial bombardment of the peaks; but a single B-1B dropping six bombs was the sum total of preparatory fires, due to a miscommunication by the planners. The militiamen, expecting massive US air support, were even further demoralized.

A small combined SF/AMF element, led by Chief Warrant Officer Stanley Harriman, broke off from the main convoy to establish a planned OP. Concurrently, the Mako 31 recce team called in an orbiting AC-130 to 'service' the al Qaeda position they had discovered, after the SEALs were spotted and engaged in a short fire-fight with the al Qaeda gun team. The gunship was then tasked to scan the surrounding area for any enemy forces with their infrared and night vision cameras. Tragically, the AC-130's navigation system was malfunctioning, and the

March 2002: the rugged summit of Takur Ghar, with the snow-covered floor of the Shah-e-Khot Valley beyond. In the original photo it is possible to make out, on the streak of snow at 4 o'clock from the single cross-shaped tree on the center skyline, 'Razor 01', the abandoned MH-47E Chinook of the Ranger quick-reaction force. (DOD/USSOCOM photo)

crew identified and plotted Harriman's small column in error. After being cleared to engage, the AC-130 struck. Harriman received a fatal fragmentation wound, two other SF were wounded, and several AMF were killed and many wounded before the AC-130 ceased fire after being informed by AFO of the 'blue-on-blue'. Soon afterwards, the main element of TF Hammer were engaged by effective mortar fire from al Qaeda positions on the slopes; this broke their unit cohesion, and the AMF scattered and refused to advance.

With no opportunity to alter timings, the Chinooks of the 101st Abn began their air assault into the Shah-e-Khot. As the grunts de-bussed they were engaged by heavy mortar and small arms fire, pinning them down. The assigned Apaches attempted to suppress enemy mortar teams, but ran into a wall of RPG and 12.7mm fire, with one gunship losing all its electronics to an RPG hit. It was now estimated that there were between 750 and 1,000 al Qaeda fighters in and around the Lower Shah-e-Khot – a far cry from the original estimates.

The grunts of TF Rakkasan and the SF operators with Hammer fought all day, while the AFO OPs called in continuous close air on al Qaeda weapon positions and the Apaches valiantly protected the exposed troops. Only one 120mm mortar had been deployed by the 10th Mountain's troopers and, whilst effective, it soon ran out of ammunition, forcing the grunts to rely on air to suppress the enemy indirect fires. Eventually, at nightfall, the most exposed Rakkasan elements were exfiltrated after suffering numerous wounded.

At AFO, alarming news was received from the leadership of TF 11: command of the AFO component of 'Anaconda' was to be handed over to the newly arrived DEVGRU element, TF Blue. Apparently more for political than any operational reasons, TF 11 also demanded that two DEVGRU recce teams be inserted into the battle on the evening of 3 March (callsigns Mako 30 and Mako 21).

Takur Ghar

A hastily drawn plan called for the MH-47 insertion of both these SEAL elements into the valley, with Mako 30 landing on Takur Ghar, a towering peak with commanding views of the Shah-e-Khot. After mechanical difficulties with the first pair of Chinooks, the teams eventually took off in the early hours of 4 March. As the 160th SOAR ship callsign 'Razor 03' approached Takur Ghar, an AC-130 scanned the peak and reported no hostiles present. The CAG operators at AFO had advised Mako 30 to insert some 1,300m off-set from the peak, taking into consideration the al Qaeda OP and gun position already discovered by Mako 31; but the TF Blue element apparently ignored this advice.

As Razor 03 touched down on Takur Ghar, the Chinook was struck by an RPG and 12.7mm fire. A DEVGRU operator, PO 1st Class Neil Roberts, fell from the open ramp as the MH-47 attempted to escape. Leaking hydraulic fluid, the crippled Chinook made an emergency landing several kilometres away and awaited rescue. Retrieving the missing PO Roberts was now the pressing objective; Mako 30 were picked up by the now empty Razor 04, which had successfully inserted Mako 21, and lifted onto the peak. The combined DEVGRU/STS team were immediately pinned down, and called for the TF 11 quick-reaction force (QRF) – a team of Rangers and attached STS based at Bagram. Mako 30 broke contact, and withdrew into cover under a rocky overhang.

The QRF launched immediately in two more 160th SOAR Chinooks, Razor 01 and Razor 02. The lead helicopter, Razor 01, was vectored in to land on the peak, unaware of the RPG and DShK threat and of the fact that the SEALs had actually broken contact. Razor 01 was engaged by intense RPG, 12.7mm and small arms fire as soon as it arrived, and was forced to crash-land when an RPG destroyed one of its engines; three Rangers and a crewman were killed immediately by small arms fire. The other Rangers and STS operators broke clear from the stricken aircraft and began engaging entrenched al Qaeda defenders.

Razor 02 landed its team of Rangers at the off-set HLZ, from where they began the arduous climb to the peak. The STS team and ETAC attached to the Razor 01 Rangers called in numerous 'danger close' airstrikes to keep the enemy at bay until the second half of the Ranger QRF could negotiate the climb and link up. Together they used classic infantry tactics to fight through and kill the al Qaeda elements on the peak; but the re-united Ranger QRF were soon engaged by al Qaeda reinforcements who attempted to retake Takur Ghar. An Australian SASR OP on a nearby mountain assisted by calling in continuous airstrikes on these reinforcements. Eventually, after 16 hours of pitched combat, the Rangers and Mako 30 were extracted that night. Sadly, efforts to locate and rescue PO Roberts were in vain. The SEAL appears to have died soon after falling from the Chinook; despite putting up a ferocious resistance, he was overcome by sheer weight of numbers.

A memorial at Bagram air base for the seven special operators who died during the battle for Takur Ghar in March 2002 – the traditional Airborne arrangement of helmet, rifle and jump-boots. (Courtesy 'JZW')

A new plan was now hatched to relieve the embattled Rakkasan units still in the valley. The 2/187th Inf air-assaulted into the east of the valley on 4 March and immediately attacked the heights under heavy gunship cover; 3d Bn were dropped into the north of the valley, with the objective of clearing through and linking up with the stranded forces. Supported by 16 Apaches, five Marine Cobras and several USAF A-10 Thunderbolts, the Rakkasans methodically worked their way through the Shah-e-Khot, eventually clearing an estimated 130 caves and 40 buildings.

The exhausted Rakkasans were replaced on 12 March by fresh elements from 10th Mtn Div, who continued to clear the southern end of the valley. Task Force Commando – consisting of units drawn from 10th Mtn and the Canadians of 3rd Bn/PPCLI – were airlifted in on 14 March to conduct SSE operations. AFO teams reconnoitered into the nearby Naka Valley, hunting for al Qaeda escapees, but they came up empty-handed. Operation 'Anaconda' officially ended on 19 March.

Payback

On 17 March, TF 11 at Bagram received real-time intelligence from an RQ-1 Predator UAV showing a group of three vehicles driving at speed in the Lower Shah-e-Khot towards the Pakistan border. The two Toyota 4Runners and a Hilux, travelling in daylight, attracted a mixed team from CAG and DEVGRU (along with an attached British SBS operator) in the 160th birds that were kept on strip alert for just such an eventuality.

The three MH-47Es carrying the TF 11 team, and two MH-60Gs carrying a Ranger security team, flew up behind the small convoy at below 50 feet, and the lead Chinook levelled out and landed on the road directly in front of it. As the occupants leapt from their vehicles and aimed their weapons, the door-gunner opened up with his 7.62mm minigun, cutting down a number of the al Qaeda fighters. The second Chinook overshot the column and raked it with minigun and M249 fire from the ramp. The TF 11 operators added their fire to the helicopter's weapons, having earlier gained permission to punch out the Plexiglas side windows to enable them to fire their M4s and SR-25s from inside the fuselage.

An Australian SASR patrol, showing the heavy firepower carried by the LRPV: a Mk 19 AGL in the "turret" ring mount, a GPMG on the passenger side, and a Minimi SAW (known as the F89 in SASR use) and an M136 SMAW within easy reach of the driver. See also page 54. (Australian Defence Forces photo).

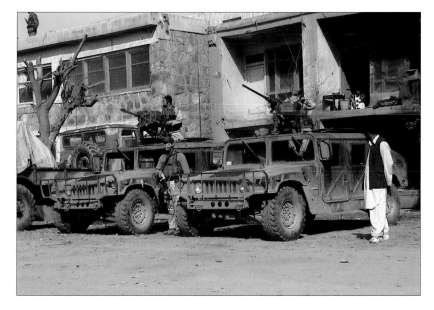

An excellent view of two up-armored HMMWVs, the left one mounting a Mk 19 AGL and the right a .50cal M2. One ODA member explained that the lead vehicle in a column usually had a Mk 19, the rear one – the 'caboose' – a .50cal M2, and the others M240s or M249s; extra ammunition and Claymores were also carried in the Humvees. In fact, few SF Humvees are up-armored; SF prefer to rely on speed, arguing that the extra armor weighs the vehicle down to an unacceptable level, though most teams will have an M1114 armored version available for special tasks. (Courtesy 'JZW')

As the third Chinook passed overhead, its minigun only managed a short burst before it jammed. A 160th SOAR flight medic and former Ranger took over, firing his M4 while the stoppage was cleared, and killing the driver of one of the SUVs as he tried to reverse out of the kill zone. A fourth vehicle had driven into a wadi some distance behind the convoy; one of the Chinooks hovered over it until positive identification could be made that the occupants were non-combatant civilians. The other Chinooks landed in cover nearby, and the operators took up positions overlooking the convoy while the Rangers orbited nearby in their Pave Hawks. As the al Qaeda survivors attempted to reach cover they were caught in a devastating ambush by the CAG and DEVGRU operators. It was all over in the space of a couple of minutes: 16 al Qaeda lay dead or dying in the dust, and two wounded prisoners were taken.

As the TF 11 operators cleared through and examined the bodies for intelligence, they confirmed that all were foreign fighters – Arabs, Chechens and Uzbeks; one male corpse was disguised in a woman's *burkha*, and another was wearing a suicide belt device. The Americans also recovered an M4 suppressor and US fragmentation grenades that were subsequently traced to the Ranger QRF which had landed on Takur Ghar, and a Garmin GPS which was confirmed as lost there by a member of the 160th SOAR.

UNITED KINGDOM SPECIAL FORCES

The first UKSF unit deployed in support of 'Enduring Freedom' was a two-squadron grouping from 22SAS in mid October 2001. A and G Sqns, both having completed desert training in Oman, were given the nod by Director Special Forces; D Sqn were on standby duty as Hereford's resident anti-terrorist (Special Projects) team, and B Sqn were on long-term overseas training. Both chosen squadrons were reinforced with personnel from the two SAS Territorial Army regiments (21 and 23SAS).

A and G deployed initially to the northwest of Afghanistan to conduct a series of reconnaissance taskings known as Operation 'Determine'. The SAS soldiers had assumed that they would be involved in direct-action operations against high-value targets, or supporting the Northern Alliance in much the same way as the US Army ODAs, and were disappointed to be given a rather more mundane recce role resulting in zero enemy contacts. After a fortnight both squadrons returned to Credenhill.

On 10 November, C Sqn, SBS inserted into the recently captured Bagram air base. Teams from C Sqn, reinforced with individual members from X and Z Sqns (and at least one SEAL operator on secondment), were soon deployed either to work alongside TF Sword in the Shah-e-Khot Valley, or with Dostum's forces around Mazar-e-Sharif.

In mid November 2001, A and G Sqns 22SAS were re-inserted into Afghanistan covertly through Bagram (Operation 'Blood') while media attention was focused on their SBS and RM colleagues. This time, allegedly after political intercession by then-Prime Minister Blair himself, the SAS had been given a direct action task – the destruction of an al Qaeda opium-processing plant. Whether this was a good fit for their capabilities is open to question; some commentators believe that the mission was more suited to light infantry such as the Parachute Regt – and indeed, the operation would indirectly lead to the later formation of the Special Forces Support Group (SFSG).

Photographs of UK Special Forces in Afghanistan are not available, for reasons of security. The relevance of this photo is simply the weapon – an M249 SAW featuring the collapsible Para stock and a 200-round plastic assault pack – which is also used by UKSF. This operator is in fact an American CIA officer from the Special Activities Division attached to an Army Special Forces ODA. He wears civilian clothing apart from the tri-color DCU trousers; note the MBI tactical radio in his right cargo pocket. (Courtesy 'JZW')

Operation 'Trent'

This became the largest 22SAS operation in history, with both squadrons tasked to assault an opium-processing facility 250 miles southwest of Kandahar, close to the Pakistan border. Intelligence indicated that the site was defended by between 80 and 100 al Qaeda, with trench-lines and several bunkers.

Incredibly, 22SAS – highly trained in night operations – were ordered to assault the complex in full daylight; this timing had been mandated by CENTCOM and was influenced by the availability of air assets, of which only one hour of close air support was to be provided. The timings also meant that the squadrons could not carry out Close Target Reconnaissance (CTR) or establish OPs to gather much-needed intelligence. Despite these restrictions, the feeling within UKSF was that if the CO of 22SAS declined this inadequately prepared operation, little else would be passed his way.

A landmark in regimental history was made during 'Trent' – the first wartime HALO parachute jump. An eight-man patrol from G Sqn's Air Troop were inserted at night to test the ground composition of a barren desert site in Registan in preparation for the landing of the main assault force in their USAF C-130 Hercules. Later that day the fleet of C-130s touched down, each aircraft only for long enough to disgorge the SAS; the men of A and G Sqns 'de-bussed' by driving off the ramps as the planes trundled along the desert strip. The 40 vehicles – 38 'Pinkie' Desert Patrol Vehicles (DPVs) and two logistics vehicles, plus eight outriders on Kawasaki dirt-bikes – soon formed up and set off for the target.

An early setback soon struck, with a Pinkie breaking down with engine problems not far from the landing site; this vehicle had to be left behind with its three-man crew to protect it until they could be recovered on the way out, as the assault force exfiltrated. With the motorcycle riders covering the front, rear and flanks of the convoy, the force drove to the identified Forming Up Point and split into two elements: the main assault force (A Sqn) and the Fire Support Base (G Sqn). The FSB's task was essential, particularly in view of the lack of artillery fires and the extremely limited nature of the close air support; its teams were armed with vehicle-mounted GPMGs, .50cal M2s and Milan ATGMs, along with 81mm mortars and Barrett M82A1 sniper rifles for precision support.

The air support arrived on time and delivered their bombs on the facility, signalling the start of the attack; A Sqn advanced, firing their weapons as they drove across treacherous terrain before de-bussing to close on the target on foot. One al Qaeda bunker proved particularly troublesome and the orbiting US Navy Hornets were called in to destroy it with a JDAM. Soon afterwards the F-18s rolled in for their final pass before departing, strafing the al Qaeda positions with their 20mm cannon (one pilot only narrowly missed several G Sqn vehicles with an ill-timed burst).

The regimental sergeant-major (RSM) in command of the FSB joined the action, bringing up elements to reinforce A Sqn when he believed the assault might be stalling. When several hundred yards from the al Qaeda positions the RSM was hit in the leg by an AK47 round; he was the second British soldier wounded during the operation, and several other SAS troopers were saved only by their body armor and helmets.

With the bunker destroyed and teams clearing the trench-lines, the main assault force swept into the compound to mop up the few remaining al Qaeda fighters and secure the buildings for search. After just under four hours on target, both squadrons mounted up and rendezvoused with a CH-47, which evacuated the four casualties from the battle.

The siege at Qala-i-Janghi

Meanwhile, C Sqn SBS were involved in one of the most infamous incidents of the early war – the 25 November prisoner uprising at Qala-i-Janghi fort. This sprawling mud-brick complex dating from the 19th century had been Gen Dostum's headquarters until co-opted to hold prisoners from the battle for Mazar-e-Sharif. Two CIA officers, who had been deployed with Dostum's forces, were conducting initial battlefield interrogation of al Qaeda and Taliban prisoners, who had been searched only carelessly by Northern Alliance fighters. Many had concealed sidearms, grenades and knives,

A support weapon also used by UKSF, though not for its designed purpose, is the Javelin FGM-148 anti-tank guided missile (ATGM). Here a round is test-fired by a member of the Australian Special Operations Task Group. The Javelin was rushed into service for the first rotation of the SOTG, and was carried on the patrol vehicles to provide an anti-armor capability. Its excellent sighting or Command Launch Unit (CLU) is also used as a stand-alone thermal imager by SASR patrols. (ADF photo)

The reliable L7A2 7.62x51mm GPMG is used on vehicle mountings by the British and Australian SAS alike. These SASR 4x4 RSV wagons mount one for the front passenger and one for a rear gunner. The Regional Surveillance Vehicle, like the British DPV, is based on the Land Rover 110. Note too the body armour slung over the spare wheel as expedient protection for the driver; and the 81mm mortar rounds carried in the rear bed. (ADF photo)

and both officers were attacked by prisoners carrying these hidden weapons. One, former Marine Capt 'Mike' Spann, was killed, and his partner, 'Dave', barely managed to escape; he eventually made contact with CENTCOM, who relayed his urgent request for assistance to the inhabitants of the 'School House', a TF Dagger safe-house in Mazar-e-Sharif occupied by members of CAG, 5th SFG and the SBS.

A quick-reaction force was hastily scraped up from whoever was in the house at the time; since the CAG operators were deployed elsewhere, that meant part of the 3d Bn/5th SFG HQ staff, a couple of visiting USAF officers, and a small SBS team from C Squadron. An American special operator who fought at Qala-i-Janghi recalled: 'The individual in Air Force uniform was not a CCT or SF-TACP; he was a USAF lieutenant colonel who happened to be [there] when the call came in. There were not many shooters available at the time, since the next big fight was anticipated to be at Konduz, so the lieutenant colonel and [a] USAF major came along with the ad hoc team to see if they could help out. The SBS really saved the day on the 25th... All were extremely professional, aggressive, and cool under fire'.

Arriving in short-wheelbase Land Rover 90s, with L7A2 GPMGs mounted on the roofs, the eight-man SBS team, who had arrived dressed in civilian clothes and with just their carbines and pistols, deployed alongside the 5th SF Group operators. The resourceful SBS patrol commander, the late Sgt Paul 'Scruff' McGough (who tragically died in a hang-gliding accident in June 2006), immediately realized the need for heavier weapons and, with the assistance of another SBS man, he used his Leatherman multi-tool to dismount the GPMGs from the vehicles.

The prisoners who had rebelled had managed to break into the fort's armory and arm themselves with an array of small arms, light mortars and RPG launchers. The surviving CIA officer and Dostum's men were fighting a losing battle against overwhelming numbers until the QRF arrived. The Americans and SBS began fighting a pitched battle against the prisoners in an effort both to stem the tide and rescue Dave. 'Scruff' was famously filmed by a camera crew at the fort, firing a GPMG from the hip to successfully stop a Taliban charge. Dave eventually managed to escape over a wall during the night; the QRF then began to focus their attention on recovering Spann's body. The fighting continued over no less than four days. The 5th Group operators called in multiple airstrikes, during one of which a JDAM was misdirected (once again, after a battery change in a PLGR GPS unit) and slammed into the ground close to friendly positions, seriously injuring five 5th Group soldiers, and four SBS men were also injured. The special operator participant commented:

'I think we had one short bomb on Day 1 of the uprising; it landed in a field to the north of the fort and caused no casualties. The other JDAMs that day were on target in the prison area. These bombs came in 'danger close', and I appreciated the skill of the pilots and the guy who called in the drop. Day 2 is when the JDAM hit the wall of the fort and killed several Afghans and wounded some [friendlies]. That was the fault of the guy who passed the coordinates to the pilot from the ground. Apparently he sent his own position instead of the target, which was a few hundred meters away. A similar situation happened to another ODA [574] farther south, and several of them were killed.'

An AC-130 kept up the aerial barrage through that night. The following day, 27 November, the backbone of the siege was finally broken when Northern Alliance tanks were brought into the central courtyard to fire main-gun rounds into blockhouses held by diehard Taliban. Fighting continued sporadically throughout the week, however, as the last remnants of resistance were crushed. When the combined 5th SF and SBS team finally recovered Spann's body they found that it had been booby-trapped with a live grenade; this was successfully disarmed, and Spann's body would be returned to the United States.

The US showed its appreciation to the SBS by attempting to have them recognized with US decorations, but British bureaucracy prevented these awards. However, a Taliban commander's chromed PPSh-41 now sits above the stairs on the way to the CO's office in Poole, as a token of gratitude to the SBS from the 'OGA'.

After the battle of Qala-i-Janghi put them on the map the SBS went on to carry out more work with both TF Sword and the OGA; but 22SAS were not so lucky. Following Operation 'Trent', A and G Sqs were again deployed on reconnaissance tasks in the Dasht-i-Margo desert, before returning to Hereford on 14 December 2001. Small numbers from both 21 and 23SAS (TA) continued close protection tasks for members of SIS ('MI6') in country, but for many 'the Regiment's' first taste of the War on Terror was somewhat less than satisfactory.

OTHER COALITION SPECIAL OPERATIONS FORCES

Australia

The Australian Special Air Service Regt's 1 Sqn deployed 60–70 men in October 2001; 1 Sqn were replaced by 3 Sqn in April 2002, and 3 Sqn in its turn by 2 Sqn in August 2002. A pause in deployments coincided with the build-up, training and deployment of an SASR squadron in support of Operation 'Iraqi Freedom'.

Their first Afghan operation was under attachment to TF 58. 1 Squadron flew in directly from Kuwait and almost immediately launched patrols, pushing upwards of 60 miles out from FOB Rhino, establishing covert OPs, and generating a tactical appreciation of the surrounding areas. Most of the later squadron groups operated under the command of TF 64, carrying out the role for which the Australian and New Zealand SAS are famed – long-range reconnaissance in hostile environments. The SASR were heavily involved in support of Operation 'Anaconda' in early March 2002, and later that month in Operation 'Mountain Lion', targeting al Qaeda elements along the Pakistani border near Khost; this included the longest mounted patrol by any unit during the history of OEF – 52 days' duration. The SASR later received a US Meritorious Unit Citation for actions in support of Operation 'Slipper', the Australian designation for their country's contribution to OEF.

A larger commitment followed in August 2005 with the deployment of the first Special Operations Task Group (SOTG), built around an SASR squadron with a company-strength QRF from 4th Bn/Royal Australian Regt (4RAR Commando), and operating in the troubled Oruzgan province, where the Australians now ran a PRT. A second SOTG was deployed in April 2007 for a 12-month rotation. These later deployments were more focused on direct-action operations, with the SASR 'taking the fight to the Taliban'.

Canada

Joint Task Force Two (JTF-2), the Canadian Army's tier-one SOF, deployed 40 men in December 2001 under TF K-Bar command. JTF-2 worked extensively with the TF's US elements, and due to their previous relationships with JSOC units were considered a US unit in terms of taskings. They deployed SR teams in 'Anaconda', assisted in the massive

Czech Republic: a Toyota Hilux used by the Czech SOG 'Omega', armed with a 7.62x54mm PKM on a specially built ring mount. (Czech SOG photo)

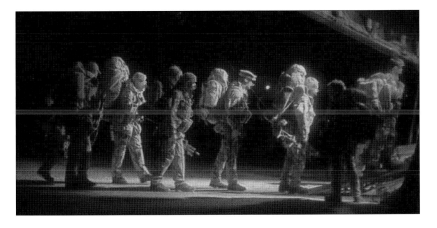

Germany: although of poor resolution, this nighttime photo is interesting as one of the only operational images of KSK operators. Seen in December 2001 as they boarded an aircraft for their first deployment to Afghanistan, they carry G36C rifles mounted with AG36 grenade-launchers. (Bundeswehr photo)

SSE at Zhawar Kili, conducted close-protection tasks, and participated in numerous DA operations – allegedly including the siege at Mirwais Hospital, where a US ODA killed a group of al Qaeda hiding in a hospital ward. JTF-2's first rotation returned to Canada in May 2002, to be replaced by a second, shorter deployment until October 2002.

Czech Republic

Since April 2007 a 35-man deployment of the Special Operations Group (SOG) 'Omega' of the Czech Military Police has been supporting the British in Helmand under ISAF, in a variety of force-protection and close protection tasks.

Denmark

The Danes deployed a 100-strong force from the Army *Jaegerkorpset* (Hunter Corps) and Navy *Fromandskorpset* (Frogman Corps) in December 2001. They primarily carried out SR tasks for TF K-Bar, including designating targets; however, they were also involved in the seizure of Taliban Mullah Khairullah Kahirkhawa, whose vehicle convoy was ambushed by heliborne Danish SOF and SEALs in February 2002.

France

It is rumoured that assets of the French *Commandement des Opérations Spéciales* were deployed before the fall of the Taliban, although the secrecy surrounding French special forces makes the UK seem positively open. It is known that 50 COS operators deployed in 2001, and 150 later deployed to replace the Italian ISAF SOF contingent in 2003, primarily conducting reconnaissance and close protection tasks. It is also known that French COS have cooperated with K-Bar elements in the south and have incurred a number of casualties.

Germany

The *Kommando Spezialkräfte* (KSK), German Army Special Forces, initially deployed around 100 men in mid December 2001 as part of TF K-Bar. Their experience was marred by a complaint commonly heard among Coalition SOF – a lack of operations. The KSK, although widely regarded as a tier-one unit, were assigned low-priority targets and reconnaissance missions; they were deployed on several SSE operations in early 2002, most often alongside the SEALs. Although nominally

31

Rare image of NZSAS personnel operating with SEALs on a long-range mounted patrol – note the Kiwi trooper at left, in distinctive desert DPMs. Behind the SEAL GMV is an NZSAS Pinzgauer 6x6 Special Operations Vehicle mounting a .50cal M2. In 2005 the Kiwis used 11 of these; earlier rotations had depended on Humvees borrowed from the resident in-country US SF Group. The SEAL GMV mounts a Mk 47 Striker 40mm AGL, and a 7.62x51mm Mk 48 Mod 0 on the nearside swing arm. The SEAL in the right foreground wears an ILC Dover half-helmet; note also the holstered SIG Sauer P226, and the New York Fire Dept sleeve patch. (Author's photo)

under OEF command, operationally the KSK has been working for ISAF since 2005, carrying out numerous operations in the vicinity of the German presence in Kabul, including a successful raid on an al Qaeda safe-house for suicide bombers in October 2006. Germany's elite counterterrorist border police unit, *Grenzschutzgruppe 9* (GSG 9), has also been deployed to the Kabul area, providing close protection to German officials and facilities.

Italy

Italy has deployed SOF from the Composite Incursion Company 'Colonel Moschin' of the 9th Para Assault Regt, and from the Navy's Operational Incursion Group. Italian SOF has not been placed under either CJSOTF or overall OEF command, however, being limited solely to support of the Italian ISAF Task Force 'Nibbio', for which they carry out local force protection and reconnaissance tasks. However, the Col Moschin Co did work with the British SBS to rescue two Italian agents in September 2007.

Lithuania

Lithuanian SOF first deployed a 40-man group in November 2002, operating under TF K-Bar. They have been involved in SR tasks, and the special recovery of a downed RQ-1 Predator. In 2006 they saw action in the south alongside British forces.

The Netherlands

The *Korps Commandotroepen* (KCT) Viper Teams have been deployed under OEF in 2005, with 165 KCT operators backed by four Chinooks. Under the ISAF mandate, KCT have also deployed in Tarin Kowt in 2006. They have conducted SR and specialist intelligence-gathering for both the Dutch NATO contribution and ISAF command.

(continued on page 41)

1: Sergeant of an Operational Detachment Alpha, US Army SF
2: Operative, Special Activities Division, US CIA
3: Combat Controller of a Special Tactics Sqn, USAF

1: Sergeant, Combat Applications Group (1st Special Forces
   Operations Detachment-Delta), US Army
2: Petty officer, US Navy Special Warfare DEVGRU
3: Sergeant, Royal Marines, British SBS

B

1: Sniper of an ODA, US Army SF
2: Trooper, Australian Special Air Service Regt
3: NCO, *Kommando Spezialkräfte*, German Army

C

1: US civilian security contractor of a PSD
2: NCO, 1er RPIMa, French Army COS
3: Commando, *Korps Commandotroepen*, Netherlands Army

Special Forces ODA 595 supporting
Gen Dostum's Northern Alliance force
at Bai Beche, November 2001

E

JSOTF & AMF force breaching
Taliban compound, c.2003

F

New Zealand: an M4A1 used by the NZSAS, featuring elements from the SOPMOD kit – a quick-detachable sound suppressor, a vertical foregrip, the AN/PEQ-2 IR illuminator, and the 4x ACOG optical sight. It has been hand-painted all over with shades of green and brown on sand-khaki. (Author's photo)

New Zealand

The initial deployment of the NZ 1 SAS Group under TF K-Bar in December 2001 numbered around 40 men, and served for a rotation of 12 months. Two further deployments took place, in May–September 2004 and June–November 2005. The NZSAS specialize in long-range reconnaissance, both vehicle-mounted and on foot, with teams deployed in the field for upwards of three weeks at a time; they also carry out DA missions.

The NZSAS teams worked extensively with other Coalition SOF including the SEALs and 3d SF Group. In December 2004 the NZ SAS Group were among Coalition units attached to CJSOTF-South that were awarded the US Presidential Unit Citation, for conducting 'extremely high risk missions, including search and rescue, special reconnaissance, sensitive site exploitation, direct action missions, destruction of multiple cave and tunnel complexes, identification and destruction of several known al Qaeda training camps [and] explosions of thousands of pounds of enemy ordnance'. An NZSAS soldier was also awarded the Victoria Cross for New Zealand – his country's version of the supreme British gallantry award – for saving the life of a comrade during a June 2004 ambush in which one of their patrol vehicles was disabled and two NZ SAS soldiers were wounded.

One US Army special operator recalls: '[We] worked a bit with the NZ SOF; they had a reputation for going pretty hard on their DA [direct action] stuff – not really a 'hearts and minds' crew… I was with Army SF, and we definitely weren't going soft, but we paled next to the Kiwis!'

Poland: GROM operators providing security for visiting VIPs; although it is obscured here, the unit wear the unusual and recently adopted Crye Multicam pattern battledress uniform, previously only extensively used by the US Army CAG. The up-armoured GMV – a Humvee modified to SF standards – mounts a .50cal M2 in its armored turret, and a 7.62x54mm PKM for the rear gunner; note also the fuel cans in the rear rack. (Polish Ministry of Defence photo)

Norway

The Norwegian Army *Jaegerkommando* (HJK) and Navy *Marinekommando* (MJK) – collectively known as NORSOF – first deployed 78 Army and 28 Navy personnel in January 2002. They operated alongside the SEALS in support of TF K-Bar, carrying out several SSEs, and their SR teams inserted into the Shah-e-Khot to support 'Anaconda'. They have since been assigned to ISAF, and lost an HJK officer in July 2007 to hostile fire in Lowgar province.

The Norwegian counterterrorist unit *Forsvarets Spesialkommando* (FSK) carried out the successful hostage rescue of Christina

Meier, a pregnant German NGO worker, in Kabul in August 2007. No shots were fired; the hostage-takers were believed to be a criminal gang rather than Taliban.

Poland
The GROM (Operational Mobile Reaction Group) enjoys very close ties to US SOCOM, and a 40-man element deployed to Afghanistan by early 2002. During 2007, after successful earlier tours in Iraq, both the 1st Special Commando Regt and GROM deployed to Kandahar, where they are believed to be working directly under CJSOTF.

Romania
Around 40 men of the 1st Special Ops Bn 'Eagles' were deployed to Afghanistan in 2006 under direct command of OEF; little is known of their operations.

SPECIAL OPERATIONS SINCE 'ANACONDA'

After the collapse of the Taliban and the destruction or expulsion of a large part of al Qaeda's forces during 'Anaconda', and with the US military then re-aligning to prosecute Operation 'Iraqi Freedom', NATO stepped in to take over the burden of improving security in Afghanistan, establishing the International Security Assistance Force to carry out peacekeeping duties and ensure that the Taliban did not return to power. The remaining OEF forces were assigned primarily to hunting HVTs and the surviving remnants of al Qaeda.

In June 2002 a new command structure was implemented, with Combined Joint Task Force 180 (CJTF-180) taking overall responsibility for OEF operations from CENTCOM. At around the same time, the Royal Marines of TF Jacana returned to the UK after a successful but

A SEAL Team 10 Humvee-GMV mounting twin 7.62x51mm Mk 48 Mod 0 machine guns. In the distance is a park of destroyed Soviet-era armored vehicles. (Author's photo)

An ODA secure an ordnance cache: 'We stopped at an AMF compound to chat, and they said they had a few arms that they needed to ask us about... It took us the rest of the day to load it up!' Three of these operators wear *shemaghs* in black, white and grey; the armor and equipment vests are in woodland pattern. (Courtesy 'JZW')

contact-free deployment. CJTF-180 was replaced by CJTF-76, and later by its current designation of CJTF-82, which joined the NATO ISAF structure in October 2006. The Combined Joint Special Operations Task Force (CJSOTF) is now a single integrated command under CJTF-180. It is built around an Army Special Forces group, with a small element from the JSOC Task Force (formerly TF 11) not under CJSOTF command but embedded within it. The CJSOTF is not under ISAF command, although it can and does operate in support of NATO operations.

The majority of CAG returned to Fort Bragg soon after 'Anaconda' in preparation for the upcoming war in Iraq (originally due to be launched late in 2002), as did Col Mulholland's 5th SF Group with its highly prized Arabic-speakers, to be replaced in turn by the 7th, 1st and 19th SF groups.

Successes did continue, however, despite the reduced emphasis. CIA and FBI teams, almost certainly supported by JSOC, managed an HVT coup with the March 2003 capture of the al Qaeda operations officer and '9/11' mastermind Khalid Sheikh Mohammed in the Pakistani city of Quetta, close to the Afghan border.

CJSOTF operations

The Combined Joint Special Operations Task Force have continued operations, focusing on training Afghan forces, including a fledgling special operations capability. They have conducted offensive and reconnaissance operations in support of both OEF and ISAF, and have hunted enemy 'persons of interest' (POI) – 'high-, middle- or low-value targets' (HVTs, MVTs and LVTs). The commentary to Plate F, on page 63, describes the tactical character of a typical raid.

One operation carried out by members of SEAL Team 10 – Operation 'Red Wing' – took place in March 2005. A four-man SEAL SR team was inserted to pinpoint a Taliban commander known as ben

Close-up of the roof of an
SF Humvee, with an operator
'racking out' next to the .50cal
M2 mount. (Courtesy 'JZW')

Sharmak in the Asadabad region; they were tasked with identifying his presence in a local village before calling in a direct-action team from the JSOC Task Force to effect the kill/capture. Compromised almost immediately by local civilians, the SEALs were surrounded by Taliban fighters and a lengthy fire-fight began. Carrying only small arms, the team were both outnumbered and outgunned. Team leader Lt Michael Murphy (posthumously awarded the Medal of Honor), already badly wounded, heroically left cover to call in the QRF; the call got through, but Murphy paid for it with his life. Two other members of the team were also killed in the fire-fight, leaving the one surviving SEAL unconscious and knocked down a gulley by an RPG near-miss.

The QRF of eight SEALs and eight aviators from the 160th arrived at the initial infiltration site in an MH-47E, only to be caught in a Taliban ambush. An RPG round entered through the open rear ramp as the Chinook descended, blowing several men right out of the aircraft. The 160th pilots were unable to keep it aloft, and the MH-47E plowed into a mountainside and exploded, killing all on board. This was the largest single combat loss for Naval Special Warfare since Normandy. The surviving SEAL managed to evade his pursuers until he was eventually taken in by a sympathetic local villager, who risked his own and his family's lives to care for the American's wounds and hide him from the Taliban. An Army joint SF/Ranger patrol found him days later; he was flown to safety, but not before assisting the SF patrol in calling in devastating airstrikes on his pursuers' positions.

Many of the operations conducted by CJSOTF forces have also revolved around seizing munitions and clearing Taliban-controlled villages, along with the occasional SSE. A typical ODA raid was explained by an Army special operations source:

'There would be a couple of trucks of SF with ANA [Afghan National Army troops]; there might be support elements like Intel types or Psyop;

sometimes we had Predator or Spectre overwatch. We would set up a standard perimeter: overwatch, crew-served [weapon] and DM [designated marksman] positions, command-and-control, casualty collection, a holding/screening area for PUCs [Persons Under Control – prisoners], and maybe a broadcast position for the [Psyop] loudspeaker.

'Sometimes the [ANA] would just knock, but the more fun raids had the 18C [SF demolitions specialist] putting a water charge on the door and blowing it. Then the Afghans would make entry and the SF guys would follow. After that it was a standard site exploitation and screening of people in the courtyard.

'One time we had a raid on a high-walled compound in the city, with the standard outer courtyard and metal gates. We used the G-Wagens to pull up next to the wall; then we put a ladder on top, and sent some Afghans and a couple of US over the wall to open the gate – rather daring, I thought.

'On another occasion, the guys were setting up demo [to blow the door] and a bad guy on the roof woke up or somehow saw us coming. He was crawling to the edge of the compound roof over the door with his AK, and as he began to point it down at the entry team, the DM took him out.'

Sometimes the SF Operational Detachment would be ambushed while either on the way to or returning from a raid. One ODA member commented on his 'standard operating procedures' in the event of a Taliban ambush:

'The Mk 19 [automatic 40mm grenade launcher] was used to shock them so we could break contact. The SOP for us was to shock them and get out of the kill zone; dismounting and engaging was not allowed unless absolutely necessary. There just weren't enough of us to sustain a fire-fight for long, so we got the hell out and called the Rangers on QRF, or called in a gunship.'

TASK FORCE 88

Task Force Sword evolved into Task Force 11 in January 2002 – the first of the 'numbered' JSOC task forces, that would eventually carry out operations in Iraq, Somalia, Yemen and the Philippines. It was later successively renamed TF 5, 20, 121, 626, 145 and 88.

At the time of writing in late 2007 the current TF in Afghanistan (nicknamed 'OCF' for 'Other Coalition Forces', as a tongue-in-cheek wordplay on 'OGA') appears to be manned primarily by a small Navy SEAL element from DEVGRU, supported by a company-sized Ranger QRF, and air assets drawn from the 160th SOAR. The Task Force has continued with its primary task of hunting al Qaeda and Taliban 'tier one and tier two HVTs'.

For example, in late 2005 an operation into Pakistan was planned when intelligence was received that 'HVT-Two' – al Zawahiri – was attending a meeting in a compound close to the border. The plan called for a SEAL platoon to parachute in from MC-130s, using directional chutes to steer across the border, being exfiltrated by two MH-53s. The US government, wary of giving jihadist elements in Pakistan ammunition against the increasingly

An up-armoured GMV in service with an ODA at Pachaghan in 2007. The heavily armored Objective Gunner Protective Kit (OGPK) turret mounts a .50cal M2. (US Army photo/Staff Sgt Michael L. Casteel)

An ODA demolitions sergeant defuses a small IED (Improvised Explosive Device) by the roadside. This one was spotted and called in by a local Afghan taxi driver. (Courtesy 'JZW')

frail government of Gen Musharraf, wanted assurances that the SEALs would not be caught. JSOC offered to add a company of Rangers to the plan, provide a security cordon and QRF, along with a CSAR team. Frustratingly, when the MC-130 carrying the raiders was actually in the air the operation was aborted by Washington. A 2006 airstrike by Predator-armed UAVs in Damadola in the Waziristan tribal lands that narrowly missed killing al Zawahiri was allegedly guided in by Task Force operators on the ground; several Taliban and al Qaeda leaders were killed by the Predator-launched Hellfire ATGMs. A large-scale overt raid in March 2006 on an al Qaeda training and logistics facility in Danda Saidgai in northern Waziristan was credited to the Pakistani Special Service Group (SSG), but was allegedly carried out by Task Force personnel infiltrated by the 160th; scores of al Qaeda members were killed during the operation, including Imam Asad, the Chechen commander of al Qaeda in Pakistan. A similar operation in October 2006 killed up to 80 al Qaeda members in Bajaur. In March 2007 Task Force teams again allegedly entered the Pakistani tribal lands to capture two Taliban commanders in southern Waziristan. These raids are designed to be deniable, with Pakistan publicly asserting that such operations are without their knowledge or consent.

UK SPECIAL FORCES

After 2002 the United Kingdom SF presence was also reduced when the focus shifted to the Middle East. A squadron-size SBS element, with a company from the SFSG acting in a similar role to the US Rangers, has nevertheless operated in support of both the Task Force under OEF, and the resident British battle group in Helmand province under ISAF. These forces are reinforced as necessary by other JSOC and UKSF assets, although it appears that responsibility for Iraq and Afghanistan have been split, primarily between CAG and 22SAS in Iraq and the SEALs and SBS in Afghanistan.

In support of the UK battle group, a night-time raid was carried out in 2006 in Sangin, northern Helmand, to capture four key local Taliban commanders. Supported by two companies from 3 Para, a combined team of 22SAS, SBS and SFSG operators snatched the targets from their compound while the paratroopers provided suppressive fires. The UKSF team exfiltrated by vehicle to link up with a waiting Gurkha QRF, but in the event they were caught in a complex ambush sprung by waiting Taliban. For over an hour they traded fire, the Taliban firing RPGs and DShK HMGs and the British responding with the GPMGs, .50 M2s and Mk 19s mounted on their WMIK and

DPV Land Rovers. Eventually, precision airstrikes from RAF Harriers and British Army Apache Longbows broke the attackers, and the combined SF/3 Para/Gurkha force was exfiltrated. Unfortunately, two SFSG members were killed during the ambush; and of the four Taliban commanders seized in the raid, two were killed in the cross-fire while the other two escaped in the chaos.

A better result was achieved in September 2007, when an SBS team from C Sqn were involved in a complex hostage rescue alongside the Italian 'Col Moschin' special unit. Two Italian ISAF intelligence officers had been captured by the Taliban, and the joint British/Italian team was tasked with their rescue. Italian and OEF assets pinpointed the location of the hostages, and the SBS, tasked with providing a stop group, orbited in helicopters while the Italians surrounded and entered the target house. The Taliban broke out with the hostages and attempted to escape in a number of 4x4 vehicles, which were quickly disabled by shots to the engine blocks from SBS aerial snipers with AW50 .50cal rifles, circling above in Lynx helicopters. The CH-47 carrying the SBS stop group landed, and the SBS team rapidly killed all eight hostage-takers and successfully recovered both hostages; sadly, however, one later died from his wounds.

The SBS have also been involved in offensive operations for CJSOTF, graphically illustrated by perhaps their biggest coup – the killing in May 2007 of the one-legged Mullah Dadullah, a top-tier HVT and the Taliban's overall military commander. After a controversial prisoner exchange of two senior Taliban commanders (including Mullah Shah Mansoor, Dadullah's brother) for a captured Italian journalist and his Afghan interpreter in March 2007, it appears that JSOC's Grey Fox unit tracked the two Taliban with the assistance of both UKSF and RAF teams. By May they had 'housed' Dadullah at a compound near Bahram Chah in southern Helmand, and after a detailed recconnaissance the SBS elected to mount a heliborne assault on the compound on 12 May, with a squadron-sized force backed by Afghan SF. Landing from CH-47s, the SBS assaulted the compound, killing upwards of 20 Taliban, including Dadullah, in a four-hour fire-fight; SBS casualties were only four wounded.

The future of ISAF?

The French withdrew their COS contingent in eastern Nangarhar province from OEF in early 2007 after the election of President Nicholas Sarkozy, with hints that the days of French contribution to the overall ISAF mission may be numbered. Norway still maintains its presence, but its 150-strong SF contingent are restricted to operating in support of the ANA in the Kabul area. Germany has also pulled its KSK contingent from OEF, redeploying them alongside the German ISAF force in Mazar-e-Sharif – a move unpopular with the men of KSK, who had built an excellent relationship with their fellow SOF. Restrictions on the operational use of NATO member nations' forces are increasingly common, despite repeated warnings from the United States and Great Britain that such restrictions, and indeed the overall dwindling of the ground support for ISAF, may have a drastic effect on the eventual outcome of the war in Afghanistan.

The effects of an IED on an up-armoured Humvee: this caused no casualties, just minor injuries from the vehicle jumping in the air. A small C4 charge was set under about 40lb of explosives extracted from old landmines; the C4 initiator went off, but only scattered the other explosives without detonating them.
An operator who was present remarked that if the device had worked it would have caused carnage, since there were quite a number of people standing around at the time. (Courtesy 'JZW')

An ODA operator conducting an exercise in 'hearts and minds'. His slung H&K MP5A3 indicates that he is in a secure area – this sub-machine gun is used only for personal protection, not in the field. (US Navy photo/ PH2 Eric Lippmann)

WEAPONS & EQUIPMENT

One US Army special operator explained to the author: 'First trip we got stuck with M16s, [although] my teammates also had a shortie AK for close-in work. I had civilian body armor, usually worn underneath a sterile DCU top. The body armor was Level IIIA soft with standalone Level IV multi-hit plates. I had a Blackhawk chest rig that I liked – very simple: just held M16 and pistol mags, a knife and a Surefire light. Another operator added 'Nowadays, I have a bit more Gucci kit. I've got an M4 with vertical foregrip, EOTech Holosight, offset flashlight mount on the rails up front, BUIS [back-up iron sights], and a single-point sling. [My sidearm is an] M9 with Crimson Trace [laser illuminator] in a Safariland dropleg holster or Fobus paddle holster… We all carried M4s, M9s and one team member had a 203 on his M4. Typically [each man had] 310 rounds of ammo, two to four grenades, two smokes of different colors, [and for the whole team] two personal defence mines [Claymores]'.

Small arms

The primary **rifle** used by the majority of SOF in Afghanistan is the 5.56x45mm caliber Colt M4A1 carbine, and variants produced by Diemaco (now Colt Canada) and Heckler & Koch; all are descended from the CAR-15 of Vietnam War vintage. Its appeal lies primarily in the versatility afforded by the Special Operations Peculiar Modification (SOPMOD) kit. Central to the SOPMOD is the Knight's Armament Co (KAC) Rail Interface System (or 'Picatinny rail') forearm, to which accessories can be mounted – e.g. Surefire tactical lights, vertical forward grips, the AN/PEQ2 infrared target illuminator or AN/PEQ5 visible laser marker. The KAC package also includes a quick-detachable (QD) sound suppressor, and QD mounts for a shortened 9in-barrel M203 grenade-launcher. The M4A1 is often deployed with the M203A1 40x46mm GL, with a point-target range of around 150m and a variety of munitions.

A rail above the receiver, in place of the carrying handle, also takes optics, e.g. Trijicon's 4x Advanced Combat Optical Gunsight (ACOG) or non-magnified Reflex close-quarter battle (CQB) sight. The M68 Aimpoint 'red dot' sight has also been adopted by US Army and other SOF. The Trijicon Reflex has now been largely superseded by various models of the EOTech Holographic Weapons Sight (HWS), which first became popular with JSOC direct-action personnel.

Another version of the M4A1 popular with the SEALs is the Mk 18 Model 0 CQBR, a 10.3in-barrel carbine giving maximum compactness. These were famously used by SEALs from DEVGRU when protecting President Hamid Karzai during an assassination attempt in September 2002.

The outwardly almost identical Colt Canada version of the M4A1 SOPMOD is the Diemaco C8SFW. There is debate over the relative merits of the two systems, and several SOF have selected the C8SFW, the most high-profile of these being UK Special Forces. All UKSF issue the C8SFW carbine as the L119A1, often mated with the H&K under-barrel 40mm grenade-launcher and designated L17A1. The most common optics appear to be the Trijicon ACOG and EOTech Holosight. Canadian, Norwegian, Danish and Netherlands SF also favor the C8SFW.

Another variant on the M4 pattern is the Heckler & Koch HK416, which has seen operational trials in both Afghanistan and Iraq and has recently been issued to JSOC operators; it was in fact developed in close conjunction with CAG, who purchased the first 500 production weapons. The principal discriminator of the 416 is the use of a piston-driven action that reduces stoppages through eliminating much of the carbon build-up. Currently only JSOC, the Asymmetric Warfare Group (AWG) and unidentified OGA elements are carrying the HK416 in Afghanistan; a 7.62x51mm version, the HK417, is expected to be adopted by JSOC shortly.

An unusual rifle developed specifically for operations in Afghanistan was the KAC SR-47 – principally an M4A1 platform chambered for the Soviet 7.62x39mm and designed to accept AK magazines. Only six examples were produced before work on the project ceased; it is not known whether any actually made it to Afghanistan. Other rifles in common use with ISAF forces include the Heckler & Koch G36 in various guises (K & C models) by the German KSK; the FAMAS G2 by French COS elements; and numerous AK variants by the Czech, Romanian and Lithuanian SOF.

The most common **sniper rifle** is the 7.62x51mm bolt-action Accuracy International PM (AI PM); this is issued by UK forces as the L96A1, by the KSK as the G22 (in .300in Winchester Magnum), and by SASR as the SR-98, and Spanish, Norwegian and Italian SOF also carry variants. Under the British designation L115A1, the .338in Lapua AWSM version is widely used by both 22SAS and the SFSG (the .338 is considered a perfect intermediate round between the 7.62/.308 and the .50 inch).

The standard US Army-issue 7.62x51mm bolt-action M24, built around the dependable Remington 700 action, is still popular with ODAs and Rangers. At least one ODA deploying in 2002 also carried an exotic bolt-action Cheyenne Tactical in .408in caliber. The M14 was also seen in the hands of Army SOF, particularly in the early days, when it was used as a Designated Marksman Rifle (DMR), and continues under a new guise as the Mk 14 Mod 0 Enhanced Battle Rifle (EBR); this is also caried by USAF Para Jumpers.

Semi-automatic sniper platforms are increasingly employed, providing fast follow-on shots. A version of the 7.62x51mm SR-25 was carried by some of the first ODA teams in country, as the Mk 11 Mod 0; the SR-25 itself is also used by the Australian SOTG. The system is based on the venerable AR-10 and is basically an accuracy-enhanced 7.62mm version of the M16. The Mk 12 Model 0/1 has also proved its worth, particularly with Navy SF; it is essentially a 5.56x45mm version of the Mk 11, allowing ammunition commonality with the ubiquitous M4A1. The Mk 12 appears to have been born of a SEAL requirement

A poster detailing the elements of the M4 SOPMOD Block 1 accessory kit, whose rail system allows the mounting of a range of specialist sights, visible light or IR illuminators, a vertical foregrip and a grenade-launcher for indirect fire; note also the sound suppressor. An ODA member commented: 'Everyone carried M4s [with] PVS-14, PEQ-2, maybe a Surefire light, with the occasional ACOG or Aimpoint. There were guys with the full SOPMOD kit, but not everyone had them.' (Crane Division, NSWC/DOD photo)

for a compact but accurate 5.56mm sniping weapon; the original weapon, known as the SEAL Recce Rifle, was a suppressor-equipped, 16in barrel M4 with various stock and optic options.

The Accuracy International AW50, in .50 Browning, is primarily used in an anti-material and Explosive Ordnance Disposal (EOD) role. The massive Barrett M82A1 (M107, in US service) has been widely adopted by both OEF and ISAF forces; this has a range of over 1,800 metres. The SEALs are also believed to field the .50 bolt-action McMillan TAC-50. Alongside the Barrett, the AW50 is used by the KSK (as the G24), UKSF and SASR. Some OGA contractors also brought along exotic systems, including at least one AA Beowulf semi-automatic .50cal for anti-vehicle use.

Among the wide variety of **handguns** carried, the most common are the 9x19mm SIG Sauer P226 & P228, Glock 17 & 19, and H&K USP. The SIG is issue for US SEALs and is favoured by most UKSF, while the H&K is carried by the German KSK and Australian SOTG. The Glock has been 'unofficially' adopted by many units including some US Army ODAs (instead of the issue M9 Beretta), the AWG and CIA.

Some examples of the .45ACP are in evidence, principally with CAG operators and the Marine MARSOC element. The CAG .45s are custom-built by unit armorers to suit each individual, with components from the likes of Wilson, Les Baer, Kimber and others. Although the 1911 platform dominates, CAG operators have been seen carrying Glocks and USPs in both .45ACP and 9x19mm.

Sub-machine guns are a rarity, and the once-common 9x19mm SMG has been comprehensively replaced by the compact carbines firing the heavier 5.56x45mm round. The only SMGs in evidence are the H&K MP5 series, which several SOF use in the close-protection (MP5K) or hostage rescue (MP5A5 or SD5) roles. ODA members have occasionally been seen carrying MP5s, but as a personal protection weapon around FOBs and safe houses rather than in any offensive role.

Shotguns are primarily carried on raids as 'Method of Entry' (MOE) tools for demolishing locks. Some M1024s and Mossberg M590s are also used at vehicle checkpoints and in force protection roles (including with less-than-lethal rounds). The Rangers and SMUs generally use cut-down pistol grip Remington 870s with frangible rounds. One special opeator commented: 'We had sledge hammers, and the Rangers had 12-gauge compressed magnesium rounds for the hinges. A Ranger told me that he wanted to see what one of those rounds would do to a bad guy, [and] I told him that I thought they were for the doors. He said, 'Well, I'm the first guy in line, and the door isn't always locked…'.

Support weapons

US SOF use several light machine guns (LMGs), including the issue 5.56x45mm M249 SAW based on the FN Minimi design. The Minimi Para version – with collapsible stock, Picatinny rails and shortened barrel – also sees much use in modified form as the M249E4. Also on issue is the Mk 46 Mod 0, a variant developed originally from SEAL requirements; this differs from the M249E4 in having the standard M249 stock and an

improved rail system. The Mk 48 Mod 0 is the 7.62x51mm 'big brother' to the Mk 46, developed for USSOCOM by FN as something of a hybrid of the Mk 46 and the general issue M240B. It features five rails, either M249 or Para stock, and a folding bipod. The 7.62x51mm SEAL Mk 43 Mod 0 is still in Naval Special Warfare armories and was deployed as late as 2003, although the Mk 46 and Mk 48 have largely replaced this M60-based platform.

Coalition SOF including the UKSF, SASR, NZSAS and most European units use variants of the FN Minimi, the Para being the most common; Germany's KSK use the visually similar H&K MG4. The UKSF, Australian and New Zealand SAS also use the L7A2 GPMG.

All SOF carry anti-armor weapons of various types. US units are often seen with the unguided 84mm M136 (AT4) LAW, and the FGM-148 Javelin ATGM. UKSF, SASR and NZSAS have all deployed to Afghanistan

USAF pararescue-jumper of the 306th Rescue Sqn zeroing weapons at Kandahar; he carries a slung M4A1 while he examines a newly issued 7.62x51mm Mk 14 Mod 0 Enhanced Battle Rifle. Built by Troy Industries for the SEALs, the EBR is a shortened development of the trusty old M14, with a collapsible stock and a rail capability for mounting accessories. (USAF photo/Senior Airman Andrea Wright)

An SF operator puts in some 'trigger time' with his issue M9 Beretta; his slung M4A1 has been intricately painted in a flecked disruptive pattern. (Courtesy 'JZW')

ODA gunner firing a tripod-mounted 7.62x51mm M240B light machine gun fitted with an ELCAN optical sight; note (right) the spare barrel in its bag. (Courtesy 'JZW')

with the Javelin, as have the Czechs and Lithuanians. UKSF also use the LAW-80 and M136 (designated L2A1 ILAW).

Vehicles

The Toyota Hilux pickup truck is a common vehicle in Afghanistan. Most in Taliban service were illegal imports (a fact that Toyota Corp were keen

The Ground Mobility Vehicle (GMV) version of the Humvee pioneered by Army SF has proven popular, and variants have been adopted and deployed to Afghanistan by the Army Rangers, Navy SEALs and Air Force Special Tactics elements. This Ranger GMV at a forward operating base (FOB) mounts the venerable Mk 19 automatic grenade-launcher – still a potent weapon for delivering a shocking instant response to contact. Note the removal of the windscreen and doors, for instant access and exit and free use of personal small arms; and the stake-sided rear bed for carrying extra gear – both features of Special Forces GMVs. (Courtesy 'JZW')

to publicize); they were smuggled in via Pakistan, often by *talibs* from the *madrassas* (religious schools) along the border. It was also rumoured that Usama bin Laden himself had presented a large number of these vehicles, purchased in Dubai, to the Taliban leader Mullah Omar in the years preceding '9/11'. The Hilux perfectly suited the tactical style of the Taliban, and was used both as a form of light APC – with fighters shooting from the rear bed – and as a more traditional 'technical' with a crew-served weapon mounted there. The Hilux appears to have been the preferred model for the common Taliban fighter, while the leadership operated in 'higher-end' vehicles: Mullah Omar had been seen in a white Chevrolet Suburban, while bin Laden and the al Qaeda leadership favored air-conditioned Toyota Land Cruisers.

Coalition SOF followed the enemy's lead and used locally procured pickups and Land Rovers to blend in with the Northern Alliance. As more teams arrived Toyota Tacomas started to appear, purchased directly by USSOCOM from Toyota North America, although some units also made individual purchases through local US dealerships. These Tacomas, often sporting a mounted machine gun, were termed 'tactical vehicles' by USSOCOM. A small number of armoured Mercedes G-Wagens were also donated to OEF by Norway and used by the ODAs. A US special operator who served extensively with the early ODA teams recalled: 'We had a mix of G-Wagens and Toyota pickups – all of the pickups had an improvised weapons mount welded just behind the cab. Crew-served [weapons] were 240s, a couple of SAWs, [and] the team guys actually had a PKM mounted on one of their trucks.'

The HMMWV, although not originally popular with Army SF, has seen increasing use, customized to the standard known to the ODAs as ground mobility vehicles (GMVs). Most have swing arms on the driver and passenger side doorframes to mount M240s or M249s, and all have a ring mount on the roof for a heavier support weapon – generally the .50cal

A close-up view of the Mk 19 mounted on an up-armored Humvee; note, on the open plate, the local field-expedient camouflage finish of small, closely spaced mid-brown 'curls' on a sand-khaki ground. The operator wears the SPEAR plate-carrier vest in woodland pattern, with a medical pouch attached to the upper back. (Courtesy 'JZW')

M2 or 40mm Mk 19. Perhaps surprisingly, most SF HMMWVs do not feature the up-armour kits seen on regular Army vehicles, since they prefer speed to extra protection. Most of the GMVs have the windscreen, side windows, and even the forward two doors removed to allow firing of personal weapons from inside. They also feature extra external carrying racks to store the myriad equipment with which an SF ODA deploys.

Most SOF units also have specialist vehicles dictated by their particular needs. The SEALs rescued from storage their Chenowth Desert Patrol Vehicles (DPV), the famous armed dune buggy, and deployed an upgraded version in limited numbers in Afghanistan. The G-Wagen is used by the KSK as the *Aufklärungs und Gefechtsfahrzeug* (AGF), mounting two forward 7.62x51mm MG3s and either an M2 .50cal or GMG in the ring mount; KSK have also operated in US GMVs. The Italian SF attached to ISAF have been seen in modified Land Rover 90s. All-terrain vehicles (ATVs), similar to civilian quad bikes, are also popular. The SMUs of JSOC have procured specialist vehicles suited for their unique mission profiles. Along with customized GMVs and ATVs, CAG use a modified 6x6 Steyr-Daimler-Puch Pinzgauer; this Pinzgauer Special Operations Vehicle is also used by NZSAS.

UKSF deployed with their distinctive Desert Patrol Vehicles (DPV) based on the long-wheelbase Land Rover 110. Still known widely as 'Pink Panthers', these in fact lost their distinctive salmon-colored desert paint jobs as long ago as the 1970s, but the 'Pinkie' title has stuck. In Afghanistan they were most famously deployed by A & G Squadrons of 22SAS during Operation 'Trent'. The current generation of the DPV

A handsome view of an SASR Perentie 6x6 Long Range Patrol Vehicle; in addition to the mounted GPMG and M2, note the two Javelin ATGMs carried in the rear bed, on top of the load of bedrolls, MRE rations and other kit for an extended mission away from base. This LRPV is finished in sand-khaki with a widely spaced camouflage pattern of faded sage-green and pale chocolate-brown stripes. The trooper wears the Australian DPDU desert camouflage uniform, the matching cap having a distinctive long, broad sun-curtain behind. (ADF photo)

generally mounts an L7A2 GPMG on the passenger side of the open cab and a heavy weapon on its rear WMIK-style turret ring. 22SAS have used a wide range of support weapons on this platform, including the 40mm Mk 19 and H&K GMG automatic grenade-launchers; both twin- and single-mount .50cal M2 HMGs; twin L7A2 GPMGs; and Milan ATGMs. (The recently introduced H&K GMG is also in use by the SEALs and US Army, as the Mk 47 Mod 0 Striker.)

The Australian SASR have their distinctive six-wheeled Perentie Long Range Patrol Vehicles (LRPV), alongside their version of the DPV – the RSV or Regional Surveillance Vehicle, also used by 4RAR. Both of these platforms offer similar weapons capabilities to the UK versions.

UKSF are phasing out the legendary DPVs in favour of the new 4x4 Supacat Special Operations Vehicle (SOV), a version of which will also be adopted by SASR as the Nary SOV – named in honour of fallen SASR WO2 David Nary.

Air assets

The 160th SOAR operate several types. The MH-47E Chinook povides heavy lift for both personnel and cargo. The MH-60K and MH-60L Pave Hawks – heavily modified Black Hawks – carry out patrol insertion and extraction, while the MH-60L Direct Action Penetrator (DAP) acts as a gunship and armed escort. The Little Birds, the AH-6J and MH-6J, also act as gunships and transports respectively. In addition to the 160th, both US and Coalition SOF are supported by the USAF's Special Operations Squadrons flying an impressive array of types, from the MC-130 Combat Talon II and MH-53 Pave Low III through to the fearsome AC-130U Spectre.

The USAF's Rescue Squadrons provide pararescue coverage for downed airmen and emergency casualty evacuation (casevac) with their HC-130s and HH-60G Pave Hawks. The subject of one such emergency casevac was an Australian, Sgt Andrew Russell, badly wounded when his vehicle struck a Russian anti-tank mine close to the Iranian border in Helmand province, during a covert recce mission by a five-man 1 Sqn SASR patrol with an attached USAF CCT. Russell was losing blood fast; his patrol medic used his advanced skills to keep him alive while the others established communications via an orbiting AWACS. An on-call HC-130 carrying an experienced pararescue-jumper team from the USAF's 38th Rescue Sqn arrived overhead; at great personal risk, the three-man PJ team conducted a night HALO jump directly into the area of the unmarked minefield, guided only the SASR patrol's IR strobes,

ABOVE RIGHT **The popular and versatile SF Polaris 'Gator' 4x4 All Terrain Vehicle; customized SF versions had IR headlights, while CAG drove 'stealth' versions featuring extensive noise-reduction modifications. Most US special operations forces use ATVs in both 4x4 and 6x6 configurations; apart from the Polaris the ATV Corp's Prowler is also popular. Capable of carrying upwards of 1,000lb of equipment, ATVs have also proven their worth with Coalition units including the Australian SASR, who have used them extensively in Afghanistan. (Courtesy 'JZW')**

ABOVE LEFT **Members of the Czech SOG 'Omega' unit, wearing the distinctive streaked Czech desert camouflage uniform, ride a heavily laden ATV with a rear-mounted AGS-17 automatic grenade-launcher. (Czech SOG photo)**

The MH-47E heavy lift transport is able to operate in thinner air at higher altitudes than any of its peers, and so is the helicopter of choice in Afghanistan's mountains. This is the view from inside a Chinook at the left side door-gunner's position (note the M-60D machine gun), and beyond to a second carrying a Special Forces GMV as a sling load. (Courtesy 'JZW')

and quickly went to work on the casualty. Two HH-60G Pave Hawks of the 66th Rescue Sqn had been scrambled from Kandahar to rendezvous with the HALO team and extract Russell; they landed on the same strobe-marked location, and the sergeant was loaded aboard for evacuation to Kandahar. Sadly, Russell died an hour into the 90-minute flight, although the PJs were still trying to resuscitate him even as the Pave Hawks touched down at base.

APPENDIX – PRIVATE SECURITY CONTRACTORS

Commonly referred to as personal security details (PSDs), these have long been deployed in Afghanistan. PSDs tend to be either former members of SOF or highly experienced former infantry soldiers or police tactical operators. They take no part in offensive operations – their role is purely defensive, as one contractor explained: 'We are there purely to protect the principals and get them out, we're not there to get into huge fire-fights with bad guys'.

Their two primary roles are providing protective security for individuals and facilities. Several high-profile PSD teams protect key officials of the Afghan government, including the DynCorp detail which until recently protected President Karzai. Contractors are also widely employed directly by the US and Coalition governments to protect both their personnel and their sites; the US military even employs contractors to guard senior staff officers. Often, the expatriate PSD team will be supported by a locally recruited and trained guard force. One highly experienced contractor discussed his experiences:

'The stuff I've been involved with was one of two things: either escorting US government officials to meetings, or providing security at US government [non-military] compounds. The second role makes it necessary to train and supervise local national guard forces. I've done this with groups as small as 20 and as large as 250, depending what part of the country I was in. Security contractors here have undertaken PSD work, static/site security and, to a limited extent, US government/military guard force supervision, force protection and sustainment training. To me, a lot of what we do is like being a firefighter – we're prepared for the worst and we spend the vast majority of our time waiting for something bad to happen, but hoping that it won't'.

With changes in enemy tactics, including the emergence of Iraq-style EFP (Explosively Formed Projectile) explosive devices, the contractors must also alter their methods and equipment. One contractor with multiple tours commented: 'DynCorp uses great big armored Ford F350 pickups. The US government teams use armored Chevy Suburbans, Toyota Land Cruisers and Mercedes G5s. The tactical guys use up-armored Hilux pickups; in the past these were modified in the field with sheets of steel and blast blankets, but more recently they appear to have been modified at the factory with built-in Kevlar and ballistic windows.'

Along with the overt armed trucks, some teams prefer to adopt a lower-profile covert approach, using local vehicles which do not stand out. Both methods have their advantages and disadvantages, the choice being dictated by the particular job: 'When I did mobile work, it was very low-profile, single-vehicle stuff... We'd try and blend in with the locals. I've long thought that the best hard car for Afghanistan would be either a modified Toyota Corolla station wagon or a minivan.'

Equipment, too, depends entirely on the role and mission profile: 'Weapons are issued – 9mm Glock G17s and M4s. The M4s are set up so that no two are quite the same: some are 10.5in, some 14in and some 16in [barrel]. Most optics are Aimpoints or EOTechs; I have my own ACOG... I've been working static rather than mobile [recently], so I

An HH-60G Pave Hawk casevac helicopter lands in a stony riverbed to evacuate a casualty, while a Special Forces GMV provides security at the landing zone. (DOD photo)

A cherry-red Toyota Hilux
modified by the ODA with
handmade lockers, an M240B
mounted on the roll-bar, and
bullbars. This is the vehicle
pictured in close-up on page 16.
(Courtesy 'JZW')

generally like to get a 16in rifle with my ACOG, as I'm not getting in and out of cars all the time and I like the option of long range accuracy.'

Many firms provide weapons and equipment that will be familiar to their ex-military employees. Sidearms tend to be 9x19mm Glocks; rifles tend to be M4s, with some SPR platforms available, and the AKs issued to local guard forces are often used by the expatriate PSD teams in back-up vehicles. Heavier weapons are not unusual in appropriate scenarios – a team may have at least one M249 SAW or RPK (often in the hands of the 'trunk monkey' in the rear of the last wagon, to discourage any vehicles from getting too close); and on high-profile jobs M240s or PKMs are often deployed.

Whether or not the security situation stabilizes, many feel that there will be fewer future opportunities for PSDs; one seasoned contractor commented that 'The Afghan government is making a concerted effort to enforce regulations for licensing and working in this country in the security field. I think that in the next few years we will see a decline in the number of security contractors working here, mainly because the security situation will improve (I hope) and, possibly, because the potential winners in an election in the States might affect the scope of the US government/Coalition effort here (I hope not).'

SELECT BIBLIOGRAPHY

Charles H. Briscoe, Richard L. Kiper, James A. Schroeder & Kalev I. Sepp, *Weapon of Choice: ARSOF [US Army Special Operation Forces] in Afghanistan* (Combat Studies Institute Press, Ft Leavenworth, KS, 2003)

Sean Maloney, *Enduring the Freedom: A Rogue Historian in Afghanistan* (Potomac Books Inc, 2006)

Gary Berntsen & Ralph Pezzullo, *Jawbreaker: The Attack on Bin Laden and Al-Qaeda: A Personal Account by the CIA's Key Field Commander* (Three Rivers Press, 2006)

Gary Schroen, *First In: An Insider's Account of How the CIA Spearheaded the War on Terror in Afghanistan* (Presidio Press, 2005)

Christian Jennings, *Midnight In Some Burning Town: British Special Forces Operations from Belgrade to Baghdad* (ORNUK, 2005)

Max Boot, *War Made New: Technology, Warfare, and the Course of History, 1500 to Today* (Gotham, 2006)

Robert D. Kaplan, *Imperial Grunts: On the Ground with the American Military, from Mongolia to the Philippines to Iraq and Beyond* (Vintage, 2006)

Sean Naylor, *Not a Good Day to Die: The Untold Story Of Operation Anaconda,* (Berkley Publishing, 2005)

Rare view of a Ranger Special Operations Vehicle; it mounts only a single M240B on a passenger side mount, but an M136 (AT4) SMAW is carried inside. These SOVs, based on Land Rovers, have since been replaced by Humvee GMVs. (Courtesy 'JZW')

PLATE COMMENTARIES

A1: Sergeant of an Operational Detachment Alpha, US Army Special Forces

Serving with one of the initial ODAs inserted into Afghanistan in October 2001, he wears the issue tri-colour Desert Combat Uniform (DCU) with a SPEAR ECW Polartec 300 fleece, and Danner boots. The only item visible on his belt is a Gerber folding knife in a branded pouch. His headgear is a traditional Afghan *pakol*, as adopted by many of the SF operators under the relaxed standards in effect at the time, to allow the ODAs to better blend in with their Northern Alliance allies. Operators adopted the full beards grown by Afghans as a sign of male maturity; replaced helmets with baseball caps, *shemaghs* or pakols; and mixed their issue BDUs with local and civilian outdoors clothing. In late 2002, MajGen Geoff Lambert of USSOCOM repealed these relaxed standards and ordered all Army SF to shave off their beards and revert to issue uniforms – an unpopular decision, obeyed to varying degrees depending on the ODA's proximity to staff-grade officers and official photographers. This man's weapon, which he has christened *Sara Jane*, is a Mk 11 Mod 0 Special Purpose Rifle (SPR) built by Knight's Armament Corp (KAC); the scope is the Leupold Vari-X Mil-dot optic, and note also the KAC QD sound suppressor.

A2: Operative, Special Activities Division, US Central Intelligence Agency

An 'OGA' officer of the period from the insertion of the Jawbreaker teams to post-Anaconda. He wears a black civilian North Face outer layer jacket, Levis, and Merrell Sawtooth hiking boots. His chest webbing is a locally produced variant of the familiar 'Chi-Com' rig for AK47 magazines, popular across Afghanistan. The drop holster appears to be a Safariland 6304 carrying a 9x19mm Glock 19 semi-automatic. His primary weapon is a 7.62x39mm Romanian AK47 variant known as a Model 90, with

a unique side-folding wire stock. 'Sterilized' AK47 and AKM variants were issued from CIA stocks to the early SAD teams, to take advantage of easy in-country access to 7.62x39mm ammunition.

A3: Combat Controller of a Special Tactics Squadron, US Air Force

The distinctive Polartec SPEAR fleece and DCUs, worn with a civilian baseball cap, became an early identifier of ODAs and attached elements in winter 2001/2002. This USAF CCT's issue M9 Beretta sits in an issue drop holster with what appears to be a Surefire Outdoorsman flashlight in the outer pouch, and a Gemtech coiled retention lanyard fitted – an important accessory when working around vehicles and helicopters. His 5.56x45mm Colt M4A1 carbine has a 40mm M203 mounted under the barrel, an AN/PEQ-2 infrared illuminator on the forward Picatinny rail, and an Aimpoint M68 combat optic above the receiver. At his feet is a typical CCT radio, the AN/PRC-117F.

B1: Sergeant, Combat Applications Group (1st Special Forces Operations Detachment-Delta), US Army

This 'D-boy' from CAG is wearing kit indicative of Task Force Sword/TF 11 during 2001/2002. CAG operators often dressed

A Ranger sniper element mounting up for a night operation. They have AN/PVS-18 night-vision devices mounted on their MICH helmets, and woodland-pattern knee and elbow pads are worn. The sniper to the left of the image carries the big .50cal Barrett M82A1 equipped with a thermal sight. The white left armband and other patches are 'glint' IR-reflective tape, applied as an IFF (identification-friend-or-foe) measure. (Courtesy 'JZW')

in a mixture of civilian hunting/mountaineering gear and 'sterilized' issue clothing – DCUs or ACUs, or the civilian-developed Crye Multicam pattern. Here the DCU blouse bottom pockets have been removed and re-sewn onto the upper sleeves, which have been cut to T-shirt length; embroidered US flags in subdued colors have been attached to these arm pockets with Velcro. His helmet is a desert-colored MICH with cutaway ears to facilitate wearing headsets such as the Peltor's type shown, which connect to his MBI tactical radio worn on the back of the vest. His boots are the Salomon Expert Mid Lightweight Hiking model. Note also the kneepad pushed down to the ankle – only one is worn, on the knee the individual favours when shooting. He wears a Paraclete RAV vest in olive drab, as both a load-carrier and a plate-carrier for mounting SAPI plates. A drop holster holds a custom 1911 .45 pistol with a Surefire weapon light mounted under the barrel. His M4A1 has an EOTech 551 optic on a LaRue mount above the receiver and an AN/PEQ-2 above the barrel. The stock has been replaced with an LMT Crane aftermarket model, and the magazines have been fitted with Magpul pull-tabs over the base to facilitate faster magazine changes.

B2: Petty officer, Naval Special Warfare Development Group, US Navy

This DEVGRU operator in civilian clothing is illustrated as part of Afghan President Hamid Karzai's personal security detail in 2002. His Royal Robbins 5.11 Tactical Vest has proven very popular with military and contractor PSD teams, although their wide use now somewhat undermines their originally intended low profile. Although they are hidden here, the Karzai PSD carried a holstered 9x19mm SIG P226 pistol, and mini-grenades attached to their belts under the vest. He wears a covert communications earpiece with the main unit concealed within the vest. His weapon is an M4A1 with the short 10.3in CQB barrel, mounting an M68 Aimpoint 'red dot' optical sight on the rail above the receiver; it also features a Tango Down foregrip mounted under the barrel, and an LMT Crane stock – the two rubber bands halfway along the stock are a field-expedient way to secure the locking mechanism, since initial production examples had problems with closing unexpectedly.

B3: Sergeant, British Special Boat Service

The only issue clothing this SBS man wears are his British desert DPM trousers; his boots are civilian Lowas, and the jacket is the famous Snugpak Sasquatch smock. Over the Snugpak he wears a field-modified Arktis Classic chest rig in faded European DPM pattern. His weapon is the 5.56x45mm Diemaco C8SFW, fitted with a 40mm H&K AG-C side-opening grenade-launcher and mounting a 4x Trijicon ACOG optic. Not visible in the image but certainly carried in a concealed holster is a 9x19mm SIG P226 pistol, widely used by UKSF along with the compact P228, and a shortened P226 peculiar to UKSF and known as the P226K.

(Inset) The SBS beret insignia – rarely seen, since members seldom parade in full uniform.

C1: Sniper or designated marksman of an ODA, US Army Special Forces

He is depicted in summer 2002 – and obviously before the relaxed grooming standards were tightened… He wears DCU trousers, Altama desert boots, and a 'covert' armour vest; an ODA operator explained that this latter 'was crappy level IIIA armor … it had an insert place for a small trauma plate [III or IV ceramic or extra Kevlar inserts] no different to police issue. Tons of it was floating around.' He also wears Wiley X tactical goggles over his reversed baseball cap. The M24 Army issue sniper rifle mounts a 10x42 Leupold Ultra M3A telescope sight, and is painted in an impressively thorough field-expedient camouflage pattern. On his thighs are strapped an M9 Beretta in a drop holster, and a 'dump pouch', both in olive drab.

(Inset bottom) .50cal Barrett M107 semi-automatic sniper rifle deployed on its bipod, with IR illuminator above the barrel.

C2: Trooper, Australian Special Air Service Regiment

He wears the desert version of the AUSCAM uniform – DPDU (Disruptive Pattern Desert Uniform) – including the rare hooded 'SAS smock'; and note the subdued Australian flag patch on his right shoulder. Oakley ballistic goggles are worn over his matching cap with sun-curtain. His chest rig is a modular design from SORD Australia in standard AUSCAM pattern, but the trooper has painted the pouches in shades of light brown and tan to break up their outline. The olive drop holster for his issue 9x19mm Heckler & Koch USP Tactical pistol has been painted in the same way. His M4A1 mounts the M203PI grenade-launcher; SASR use the M4 (known in ADF service as the M4A5, in a curious type classification) in preference to the licence-produced Steyr AUG F-88 Australian service rifle, due to the M4's superiority in maritime environments and ability to mount accessories using the rail system.

C3: NCO, *Kommando Spezialkräfte*, German Army

This KSK soldier is wearing German-issue desert-pattern BDU; known originally as *Tropentarn* but recently renamed *Wüstentarn*, this was first issued during the UN intervention in Somalia, but the pattern colours have been refined to better match an Afghan or Middle Eastern environment. (The rare photos of men of the Danish *Jaegerkorpset* in-country are often confused with German KSK due to the similarity of Danish M/01 camouflage with German continental *Flecktarn* pattern.) His footwear appears to be Meindl desert boots; note that he wears a locally procured shemagh in dark khaki. His customized Arktis chest rig has faint streaks of sand-color painted on the olive pouches. His sound-suppressed 5.56x45mm Heckler & Koch G36K mounts an EOTech 551 HWS optical sight. Unseen from this angle is his sidearm, probably a 9x19mm USP in a belt rig.

(Inset above) KSK beret badge.

D1: US civilian security contractor of a Personal Security Detail

This contractor's helmet is the MICH in desert tan. His clothing is the commercially produced SWG Raid blouse in tan, with matching trousers, and he seems to wear Belleville 590 boots as issued by the USMC. His load-carrier is an Eagle CIRAS Land vest in 'coyote-tan' colour; note the subdued American flag and 'NKA' (No Known Allergies) patches on the Velcro ID strip at the top. His M4A1 has a vertical foregrip and ACOG sight; behind this is mounted a Docter Optics sight, which gives the shooter a CQB 'red dot' option along with the 4x magnification of the main ACOG. On his right wrist is a compass originally designed for diving, which many special operators choose to wear as back-up to their GPS systems.

D2: NCO, *1er Régiment Parachutiste d'Infanterie de Marine*, French *Commandement des Opérations Spéciales*

This operator from the French Army deep-penetration unit

A US Psyops soldier (left) attached to a Special Forces ODA wears the earlier PASGT vest in woodland pattern, and carries a standard M16A2 rifle. The AMF fighter (right) has a locally produced 'Chi-Com' chest rig and US woodland-pattern BDUs. In the background are two Afghan policemen, in dark olive uniforms with white embellishments, and white-on-kelly-green chest tape and sleeve patch; the three Afghans all carry AK series rifles. (Courtesy 'JZW')

1er RPIMa wears French-issue desert pattern trousers with a cold-weather jacket in woodland pattern, and issue desert boots; the Hatch kneepads are useful in the rugged mountains. His helmet is an older-design plastic Protec with a mount for night-vision goggles (NVG), which has been hand-painted in desert colours. The chest rig appears to be another modified Arktis model in the distinctive woodland pattern; and note the drinking tube of a hydration bladder visible over his left shoulder. The drop holster on his right thigh appears to be a standard Blackhawk CQC holster carrying an H&K USP. His 5.56x45 FAMAS G2 bull-pup assault rifle mounts an ACOG optic; some photos show hand-painted camouflage, and the AN/PEQ-2 IR illuminator.

D3: Commando, *Korps Commandotroepen*, Netherlands Army
This Viper Team operator wears the US MICH helmet with NVG attachment point; US DCU trousers; Lowe hiking boots, and an issue OD T-shirt under his load-bearing vest in Dutch DPM pattern. Note the drinking tube extending over his left shoulder from a hydration bladder mounted on his back, probably a Camelbak or Source model; and also the lead from the radio in a rear pouch to a handset clipped to the front of his vest. He sports the ever-popular Oakley M-Frame

sunglasses and Nomex aviator gloves. His sidearm, fixed sideways high on his vest, is a 9mm Glock 17 in a tan Blackhawk Serpa holster. His primary weapon is the Diemaco C8 carbine equipped with an ELCAN optical sight. **(Inset)** Shoulder insignia of NATO International Security Assistance Force.

E: SF ODA 595 supporting General Dostum's Northern Alliance force at Bai Beche, early November 2001
The Taliban force (background) were bunkered down in a mixture of poorly constructed trench lines and a few sandbagged strongpoints forward of the village, with one or two Soviet-era T-55 tanks dug into hull-down positions; the Taliban also had some 82mm mortars and DShK 12.7mm heavy machine guns. In this reconstruction three members of ODA 595 (foreground) are guiding in the B-52 strike via radio while marking the target with their SOFLAM designator. According to a member of ODA 595, one of Gen Abdur Rashid Dostum's lieutenants misunderstood the call to stand by for a signal to attack, and to the Americans' horror the mounted Northern Alliance fighters charged out across the plain prematurely, while the first bomb was actually dropping. Some of these warriors fired on the gallop, resting their AKs across their left forearms while still holding the reins in their left hands. Several Taliban mortar rounds fell among the horsemen, but the cavalry charge hit the Taliban immediately after the B-52's bombs exploded, and overran the position while the defenders were still in shock.

F: JSOTF and AMF force breaching a Taliban compound, c.2003
Raids by JSOTF personnel to seize reported 'high-value targets' (HVTs) or 'persons of interest' (POIs) were sometimes

heliborne, sometimes by vehicle. An Army special operator who took part in numerous HVT raids explained:

'A typical team consisted of Army Rangers (10 to 15, with a lieutenant in charge); 1 to 3 OGA, for obvious reasons; 2 to 5 Army SF for high-level commo [communications], explosives, linguistics, etc; and, depending on the mission, 5 to 8 AMF. We choppered out with the 160th to where the high-value target suspect was, made the hit and choppered back – or, made the hit and called in more Rangers to secure the area, as no AMF were allowed on chopper missions. Or we took Hilux Toyotas and drove out to the [area of operations] without the Rangers (they only rode in HMMWVs, but the HMMWVs were too wide to make it down many of the roads in the north). We fattened the teams with SF and/or CAG guys, and more AMF to ensure we had enough guns in these cases'.

A couple of Ranger SOVs at a forward operating base; both appear to mount .50cal M2s and to carry Javelins. (Courtesy 'JZW')

Here, the team have overwatch from a circling AH-64 Apache **(inset 1)**. As the raid goes in, the main gate of the mud-brick compound and its side wall are covered against any escapees ('squirters') by a Soviet PKM machine gun mounted in a Toyota Hilux pickup truck, manned by a member of Afghan Militia Forces directed by a US operator **(inset 2)**; and a US SF Humvee mounting a Mk 19 automatic grenade-launcher **(inset 3)**.

In the main gateway of the compound – which is a traditionally walled civilian hamlet, not a specifically military position – two SF operators are directing about a dozen AMF **(inset 4)**. Once inside, other SF soldiers of this primary entry team disarm a couple of captured black-turbanned Taliban **(inset 5)** – the aim is to take prisoners, not to kill unless unavoidable. Meanwhile, on the far side of the compound, an SF secondary entry team climb in by means of a ladder, surprising and if necessary engaging the Taliban, who rush out of the houses amidst the startled civilians.

Not shown here, but commonly employed, a sniper or designated marksman team on higher ground would be ready to provide precision fire if resistance was met.

G1: Long Range Patrol Vehicle, Australian Special Air Service Regiment

The Perentie LRPV is a six-wheel Land Rover variant named after an indigenous Australian lizard. The LRPV's top ring can mount an M2 .50cal HMG, Mk 19 40mm grenade-launcher (soon to be replaced by the H&K GMG model), or GPMGs. The front passenger side swivel mount traditionally holds a GPMG.

G2: Toyota Tacoma tactical vehicle, US Special Operations Forces

This Tacoma is representative of the range of commercial 4x4 pickups used by US SOF in Afghanistan. This example has been modified with a rear mount for the team's 7.62x51mm M240B, with attached AN/PVS-10 day-night scope.

INDEX